MASTERMINDS Riddle Math *Series*

PRE-ALGEBRA

Reproducible Skill Builders And Higher Order Thinking Activities Based On NCTM Standards

By Brenda Opie and Douglas McAvinn

Incentive Publications, Inc.
Nashville, Tennessee

Illustrated by Douglas McAvinn
Cover illustration by Douglas McAvinn

ISBN 0-86530-338-X

PRINTED IN THE UNITED STATES OF AMERICA

TABLE OF CONTENTS

What do you call laughter?

NAME_____

DIRECTIONS: Define the variable in each problem and then write an equation. Solve the problem and find your answer in the decoder. Each time the answer occurs in the decoder, write the letter of the problem above it.

1. A number divided by 6 is 3. _____18_____ (i)

2. Thirty-three more than a number is 55. _____22_____ (h)

3. Claire earned $270 last week. She worked for 30 hours. How much did she earn per hour? ___$9___ (a)

4. Jon bought 2 items that together cost $16.95. One item cost $8.95. What was the cost of the other item? ___$8___ (s)

5. The Golden Gate Bridge in San Francisco spans 4,200 feet. The Verrazano-Narrows bridge in New York is 60 feet longer. How long is the Verrazano-Narrows Bridge? ___4260___ (r)

6. In 1936, the New York Yankees lost 51 games. They won twice as many as they lost. How many games did the Yankees win? ___102___ (t)

7. Babe Ruth hit a total of 114 home runs in 1928. He hit 54 home runs in 1927. How many more home runs did he hit in 1928 than in 1927? ___60___ (e)

8. In 1988, Joe DeLoach of the United States set a new Olympic record for running the 200-meter run in 19.75 seconds. In 1936, Jesse Owens had run the 200 meter in 20.65 seconds. How much faster did DeLoach run this event? ___.90___ (m)

9. A four person relay team ran a race in 56 seconds. What was the average time for each runner? ___14___ (l)

10. Three times a certain number is 45. What is the number? ___15___ (u)

11. A swordfish, one of the fastest swimming of all fish, can swim 4 times as fast as a trout that can swim 17 miles per hour. How fast does the swordfish swim? ___68___ (b)

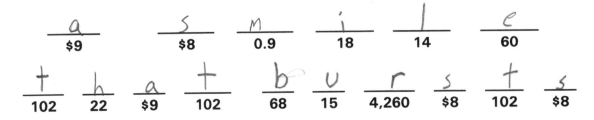

a	s	m	i	l	e
$9	$8	0.9	18	14	60

t	h	a	t	b	u	r	s	t	s
102	22	$9	102	68	15	4,260	$8	102	$8

NAME _____

2

Why is it best to call a 24-hour wrecker when your car breaks down?

DIRECTIONS: Find the value of each expression. Then find your answer in the decoder. Each time your answer occurs in the decoder write the letter of the problem above it.

1. $(84 \div 4) \div 3 =$ ___7___ (w)

2. $12 \div 3 + 12 \div 2 =$ ___10___ (i)

3. $72 \div 8 \cdot 4 \div 2 =$ ___18___ (n)

4. $(40 \cdot 2) - (6 \cdot 12) =$ ___8___ (r)

5. $2[5(4 + 6) - 2] =$ ___96___ (l)

6. $\dfrac{86 - 11}{9 + 6} =$ ___5___ (e)

7. $3[(18 - 3) + 5(5 + 7)] =$ ___225___ (y)

8. $144 \div 16 \cdot (12 \div 3) =$ ___36___ (s)

9. $\dfrac{37 + 38}{45 - 42} =$ ___25___ (a)

10. $96 \div (12 \cdot 4) \div 2 =$ ___1___ (h)

11. $(8 - 5)(5 + 2) =$ ___21___ (o)

12. $4[2(21 - 17) + 3] =$ ___44___ (t)

T	h	e	r	e		a	r	e
44	1	5		225	8	25	8	5

a	l	w	a	y	s	
25	96	7	25	225	36	21

T	o	w	i	n	g
44	21	7	10	18	36

NAME _____

Solving equations using inverse operations

Why shouldn't some cats play cards?

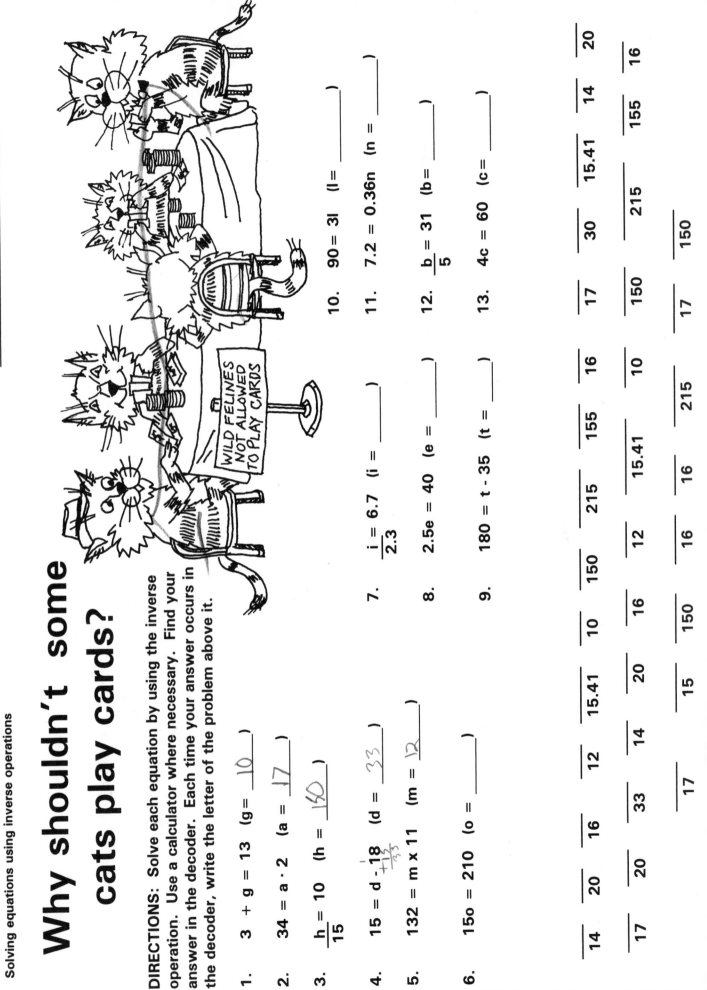

WILD FELINES NOT ALLOWED TO PLAY CARDS

DIRECTIONS: Solve each equation by using the inverse operation. Use a calculator where necessary. Find your answer in the decoder. Each time your answer occurs in the decoder, write the letter of the problem above it.

1. $3 + g = 13$ $(g = 10)$

2. $34 = a \cdot 2$ $(a = 17)$

3. $\dfrac{h}{15} = 10$ $(h = 150)$

4. $15 = d - 18$ $(d = 33)$

5. $132 = m \times 11$ $(m = 12)$

6. $15o = 210$ $(o =)$

7. $\dfrac{i}{2.3} = 6.7$ $(i =)$

8. $2.5e = 40$ $(e =)$

9. $180 = t - 35$ $(t =)$

10. $90 = 3l$ $(l =)$

11. $7.2 = 0.36n$ $(n =)$

12. $\dfrac{b}{5} = 31$ $(b =)$

13. $4c = 60$ $(c =)$

$\overline{14}\ \overline{20}\ \overline{16}\ \overline{33}\ \overline{14}\ \overline{20}\ \overline{15.41}\ \overline{10}\ \overline{150}\ \overline{215}\ \overline{155}\ \overline{16}\ \overline{30}\ \overline{15.41}\ \overline{14}\ \overline{20}$

$\overline{17}\ \overline{20}\ \overline{12}\ \overline{15}\ \overline{150}\ \overline{16}\ \overline{12}\ \overline{16}\ \overline{15.41}\ \overline{155}\ \overline{215}\ \overline{17}\ \overline{215}\ \overline{155}\ \overline{16}$

$\overline{17}\ \overline{15}\ \overline{150}\ \overline{215}\ \overline{16}\ \overline{150}\ \overline{17}\ \overline{150}$

What colors would you paint the sun and the wind?

4

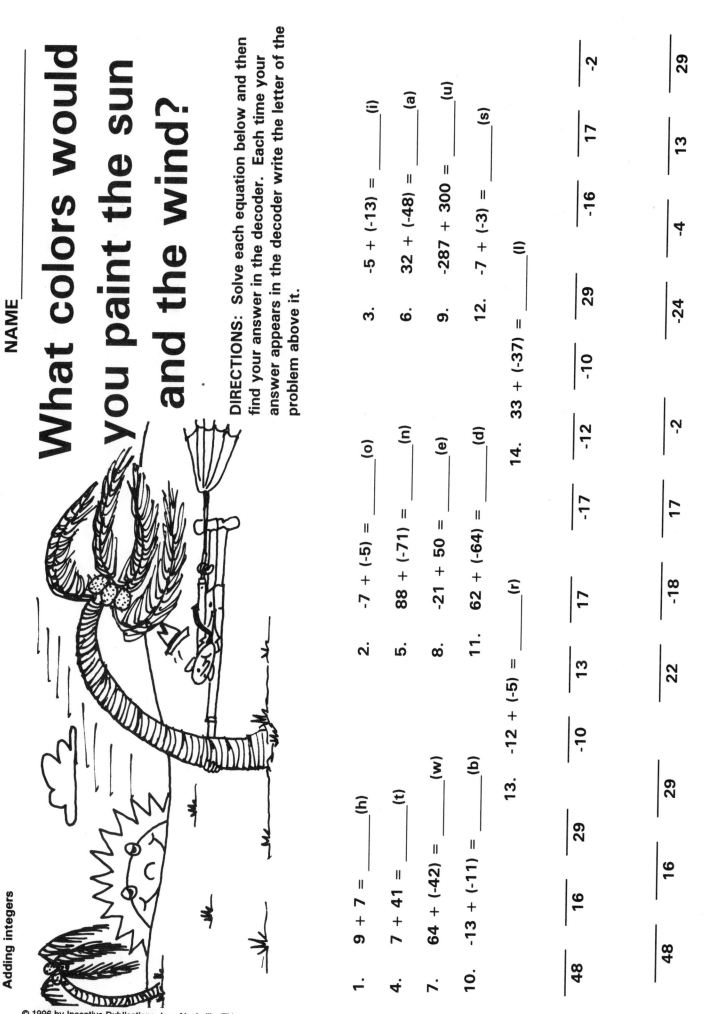

DIRECTIONS: Solve each equation below and then find your answer in the decoder. Each time your answer appears in the decoder write the letter of the problem above it.

1. $9 + 7 =$ _____ (h)

2. $-7 + (-5) =$ _____ (o)

3. $-5 + (-13) =$ _____ (i)

4. $7 + 41 =$ _____ (t)

5. $88 + (-71) =$ _____ (n)

6. $32 + (-48) =$ _____ (a)

7. $64 + (-42) =$ _____ (w)

8. $-21 + 50 =$ _____ (e)

9. $-287 + 300 =$ _____ (u)

10. $-13 + (-11) =$ _____ (b)

11. $62 + (-64) =$ _____ (d)

12. $-7 + (-3) =$ _____ (s)

13. $-12 + (-5) =$ _____ (r)

14. $33 + (-37) =$ _____ (l)

_____ _____ _____ _____ _____ _____ _____ _____ _____
-2   17   -16   29   -10   -12   -17   13   17

_____ _____ _____ _____ _____ _____ _____ _____ _____
29   13   -4   -24   -2   22   17   16   29

_____ _____
48   16

NAME_____

What did the man say when he found he was going bald?

DIRECTIONS: Solve each equation below. Then find your answer in the decoder. Each time your answer appears in the decoder, write the letter of the problem above it.

Solve each equation

1. $3 + (-13) + (-15) = d$ (d = _____)

2. $4 + (-10) + 22 = i$ (i = _____)

3. $47 + 32 + (-15) = g$ (g = _____)

4. $49 + (-18) + (-23) = r$ (r = _____)

5. $-3 + (-16) + 28 = n$ (n = _____)

6. $-3 + 12 + (-13) = a$ (a = _____)

7. $7 + 42 + (-17) = m$ (m = _____)

8. $14 + (-20) + 39 = w$ (w = _____)

9. $e = -12 + 9 + (-3) + 6$ (e = _____)

10. $y = 98 + (-99) + 99 + (-97)$ (y = _____)

11. $h = -69 + 32 + (-7) + (-16)$ (h = _____)

12. $t = 28 + (-56) + 32 + (-74)$ (t = _____)

13. $o = -11 + 8 + (-7) + 7$ (o = _____)

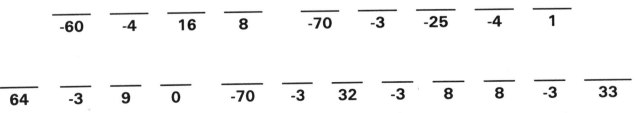

| -60 | -4 | 16 | 8 | -70 | -3 | -25 | -4 | 1 |

| 64 | -3 | 9 | 0 | -70 | -3 | 32 | -3 | 8 | 8 | -3 | 33 |

Why do golfers wear two shirts when they play golf?

DIRECTIONS: Solve each equation below, and then find your answer in the decoder. Each time your answer appears in the decoder, write the letter of the problem above it.

1.   -5 -2 = _____ l

2.   -5 - (-8) = _____ h

3.   -15 - 24 = _____ a

4.   -34 - (-20) = _____ y

5.   -17 - (-17) = _____ g

6.   -17 - (-2) = _____ s

7.   34 - (-19) = _____ t

8.   -15 - 23 = _____ i

9.   7 - 16 = _____ c

10.   -42 - 38 = _____ e

11.   -17 - (-18) = _____ n

12.   29 - 32 = _____ o

___ ___   ___ ___ ___ ___
-38   1   -9   -39 -15 -80

___ ___ ___ ___   ___ ___ ___
53   3   -80 -14   0   -80   53

     ___   ___ ___ ___ ___
     -39   3   -3   -7   -80

     ___ ___   ___ ___ ___
     -38   1   -3   1   -80

© 1996 by Incentive Publications, Inc., Nashville, TN.

Positive and negative integers

NAME_____

Record Lows and Highs in the United States

(Figures supplied by the National Climatic Data Center)

DIRECTIONS: Complete the difference in lows and highs section of this chart.

State	Record Low	Record High	Difference in lows and highs
Alabama	-27° F (January 30, 1966)	112° F (September 5, 1925)	
Alaska	-80° F (January 23, 1971)	100° F (June 27, 1915)	
California	-45° F (January 20, 1937)	134° F (July 10, 1913)	
Georgia	-17° F (January 27, 1940)	112° F (July 24, 1952)	
Montana	-70° F (January 20, 1954)	117° F (July 5, 1937)	
Nevada	-50° F (January 8, 1937)	122° F (June 23, 1954)	
New York	-52° F (February 18, 1979)	108° F (July 22, 1926)	
Tennessee	-32° F (December 30, 1917)	113° F (August 9, 1980)	
Utah	-69° F (February 1, 1985)	117° F (July 5, 1985)	
Hawaii	12° F (May 17, 1979)	100° F (April 27, 1931)	

1. Which state had the greatest difference in temperature? _____

2. Which state set both its highest and lowest temperatures in the same year?
   _____

3. Which state had the least difference in temperature changes? _____

4. Which state reported the coldest temperature? _____

5. Which state reported the hottest temperature? _____

Extension Activity: Make a graph to show the differences that you have found on this climate chart.

NAME_____

Can you discover the pattern?

DIRECTIONS: Write the next three terms for each sequence.

1. 7, 16, 25, 34 _____ , _____ , _____

2. 41, 34, 27, 20 _____ , _____ , _____

3. 13, 5, -3, -11 _____ , _____ , _____

4. 3, 4, 7, 12, 19 _____ , _____ , _____

5. 3.43, 4.77, 6.11, 7.45 _____ , _____ , _____

6. -130, -115, -100, -85 _____ , _____ , _____

7. $3\frac{1}{3}$, $4\frac{1}{12}$, $4\frac{5}{6}$ _____ , _____ , _____

8. 2.06, 2.00, 1.94, 1.88 _____ , _____ , _____

9. -16, -12, -8, -4 _____ , _____ , _____

10. 3, 9, 27, 81 _____ , _____ , _____

11. $-1\frac{1}{4}$, $-1\frac{7}{12}$, $-1\frac{11}{12}$ _____ , _____ , _____

12. 2, 4, 8, 16, _____ , _____ , _____

13. -4, 16, -64, 256, _____ , _____ , _____

NAME_____

Why isn't your nose twelve inches long?

DIRECTIONS: Solve each equation below. Then find your answer in the decoder. Each time your answer occurs in the decoder, write the letter of the problem above it.

1. (-9)(18) = _____(n)

2. (-8)(-8)(-3) = _____(i)

3. (5)(-7)(-4) = _____(l)

4. (10)(-17)(5) = _____(h)

5. -11(-7) = _____(a)

6. -8(-8)(-8) = _____(o)

7. (-6)(-4)(3) = _____(u)

8. -16(-2) = _____(d)

9. -7(30) = _____(w)

10. -6(-7)(2) = _____(b)

11. (21)(-3)(2) = _____(e)

12. 6(-3)(-5) = _____(t)

13. -3(-4)(-9) = _____(f)

| 90 | -850 | -126 | -162 | -192 | 90 | -210 | -512 | 72 | 140 | 32 |

| 84 | -126 | 77 | -108 | -512 | -512 | 90 |

Why did the invisible man go crazy?

DIRECTIONS: Solve each equation. Then find your answer in the decoder.
Each time your answer occurs in the decoder write the letter of the problem
above it.

1. $36 \div (-3) =$ _____(g)

2. $-56 \div (-8) =$ _____(f)

3. $-343 \div (-7) =$ _____(i)

4. $40 \div (-5) =$ _____(d)

5. $80 \div (-16) =$ _____(u)

6. $-91 \div 13 =$ _____(n)

7. $-100 \div -25 =$ _____(h)

8. $144 \div (-9) =$ _____(t)

9. $-200 \div (-10) =$ _____(o)

10. $-90 \div (-15) =$ _____(m)

11. $90 \div (-5) =$ _____(s)

| 20 | -5 | -16 | | 20 | 7 | | -18 | 49 | -12 | 4 | -16 |

| 20 | -5 | -16 | | 20 | 7 | | 6 | 49 | -7 | -8 |

Adding, subtracting, multiplying, and dividing integers   NAME_____

Who referees sporting events in Vatican City?

DIRECTIONS: Solve each problem and then find your answer in the decoder. Each time your answer occurs, write the letter of the problem above it.

1. -2 + (-7) = _____(o)

2. -13(10) = _____(t)

3. 15 - 20 = _____(a)

4. -15 + 30 + 20 + (-11) = _____(n)

5. -5(-8)(3) = _____(e)

6. -2 + (-8) + 6 = _____(m)

7. -17(-8) = _____(l)

8. -12 ÷ (-6) = _____(i)

9. 61 + (-33) + (-20) = _____(r)

10. -10 - (-2) = _____(h)

11. -36 ÷ 6 = _____(p)

12. 18(-9) = _____(y)

13. -48 ÷ (-6) + 12 = _____(u)

 ‾‾‾‾‾   ‾‾‾‾   ‾‾‾‾‾   ‾‾‾‾   ‾‾‾‾   ‾‾‾‾‾   ‾‾‾‾‾
  -130   -8   120   -8   -9   136   -162

 ‾‾‾   ‾‾‾   ‾‾‾   ‾‾‾   ‾‾‾‾   ‾‾‾‾   ‾‾‾   ‾‾‾   ‾‾   ‾‾   ‾‾‾‾
   8   -9   -4   -5   24   20   -4   -6   2   8   120

NAME _____

Why is an island like the letter t?

DIRECTIONS: Solve each equation below, and then find your answer in the decoder. Each time your answer appears in the decoder, write the letter of the problem above it.

1. $f + (-7) = 16$ (f = 23)

2. $t + (-11) = -22$ (t = ___)

3. $o + (-8) = 7$ (o = ___)

4. $43 + a = -16$ (a = ___)

5. The best deal Scott could find on a new truck was $8,950. This price also included a $659 option package. What was the price of the car without the option package?   Price = w   (w = ___)

6. You recently purchased a CD player and a set of speakers for $875. If the speakers were $257, how much did you pay for the CD player? CD player = b   (b = ___)

7. $i + (-21) = -58$ (i = ___)

8. $r + (-18) = 25$ (r = ___)

9. $44 = d + 64$ (d = ___)

10. $e + (-3) = 18$ (e = ___)

11. $15 = h + 42$ (h = ___)

12. $n + 14 = -32$ (n = ___)

13. $-12 + l = -38$ (l = ___)

14. $18 + m = -57$ (m = ___)

$618	15	-11	-27	-59	43	21	-37	-46	-11	-27	21
-75	-37	-20	-26	21	15	23	$8,291	-59	-11	21	43

f

© 1996 by Incentive Publications, Inc., Nashville, TN.

NAME _____

Solving equations: x - b = c

Where did Abraham Lincoln live?

DIRECTIONS: Solve each equation. Then find your answer in the decoder. Each time your answer occurs in the decoder write the letter of the problem above it.

1. $b - 16 = 32$ b = _____
2. $h + (-13) = 6$ h = _____
3. $v - (-17) = 13$ v = _____

4. $43 = y - (-48)$ y = _____
5. $t + (-8) = -31$ t = _____
6. $s - (-49) = -36$ s = _____

7. $d - 27 = -64$ d = _____
8. $i + (-8) = 26$ i = _____
9. $-18 = a - 76$ a = _____

10. $e + (-14) = 21$ e = _____

11. Ryan had $145.00 when he started shopping for school clothes. After purchasing a shirt, a pair of jeans, and a sweater he had $32.00 left. How much did he spend?   _____ = u

12. Katie made a deposit of $125.00 for a summer softball camp. She still has $250.00 to pay. How much was the total fee for Katie's softball camp?   _____ = r

13. Phillip is representing his school in a quiz bowl. After answering a 150-point question correctly, his score is -200. What was his score before he answered the question?   _____ = g

34	19	58	-37	35	19	34	-85	-350	35	-23	19	-5	-85	48	$113	$375	-350
58	-37	58	-4	$375	35	-85	$375	-350	-23	19	35	35	$375	$375	35

Solving equations: ab = x

NAME_____

What is the favorite dessert of boxers and carpenters?

DIRECTIONS: Solve each equation below. Then find your answer in the decoder. Each time your answer occurs in the decoder, write the letter of the problem above it.

1. $-8h = 64$ h = _____

2. $-3n = -36$ n = _____

3. $165 = -11t$ t = _____

4. $4a = -64$ a = _____

5. $-7u = 91$ u = _____

6. $-14e = -182$ e = _____

7. $17d = 136$ d = _____

8. $-60 = -15o$ o = _____

9. $-14c = -98$ c = _____

10. If Jon weighs four times as much as his baby brother, and his brother weighs 21 pounds, how much does Jon weigh? _____ = k

11. Morgan makes $15.00 per week babysitting. Her older sister makes 5 times as much as she does working as a cashier at the local supermarket. How much does her sister make? _____ = p

___ ___ ___
-15   -8   13

___ ___ ___ ___ ___
$75   4   -13   12   8

___ ___ ___ ___
7   -16   84   13

NAME _____

What is the first part of a geography book called?

Solving equations- $\frac{x}{a} = c$

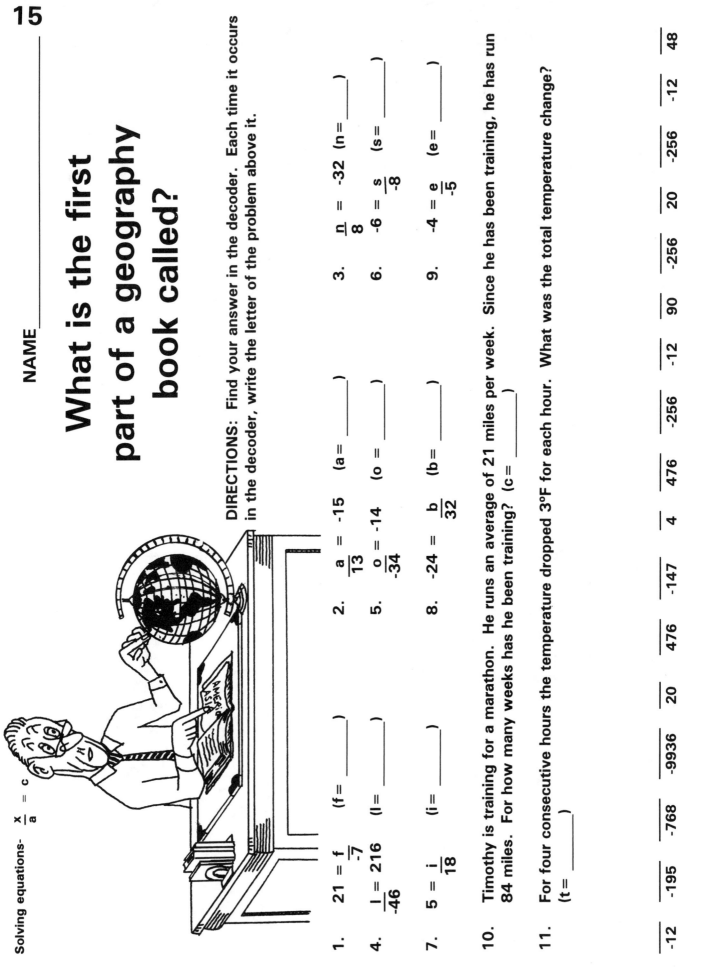

DIRECTIONS: Find your answer in the decoder. Each time it occurs in the decoder, write the letter of the problem above it.

1. $21 = \frac{f}{-7}$ (f = _____)

2. $\frac{a}{13} = -15$ (a = _____)

3. $\frac{n}{8} = -32$ (n = _____)

4. $\frac{l}{-46} = 216$ (l = _____)

5. $\frac{o}{-34} = -14$ (o = _____)

6. $-6 = \frac{s}{-8}$ (s = _____)

7. $5 = \frac{i}{18}$ (i = _____)

8. $-24 = \frac{b}{32}$ (b = _____)

9. $-4 = \frac{e}{-5}$ (e = _____)

10. Timothy is training for a marathon. He runs an average of 21 miles per week. Since he has been training, he has run 84 miles. For how many weeks has he been training? (c = _____)

11. For four consecutive hours the temperature dropped 3°F for each hour. What was the total temperature change? (t = _____)

-12	-195	-768	-9936	20	476	-147	476	4	-256	-12	90	-256	20	-256	-12	48

Using exponents

Why are ghosts
lonely all the time?

DIRECTIONS: Determine the value of each number named by the whole number and its exponent. Find your answer in the decoder, and each time your answer occurs in the decoder write the letter of the problem above it.

1. 2^4 = _____ (v)

2. 3^3 = _____ (o)

3. 8^4 = _____ (h)

4. 1^5 = _____ (e)

5. 6^3 = _____ (y)

6. 7^3 = _____ (n)

7. 11^2 = _____ (a)

8. 10^4 = _____ (g)

9. 5^4 = _____ (t)

10. 12^3 = _____ (d)

11. 2^6 = _____ (b)

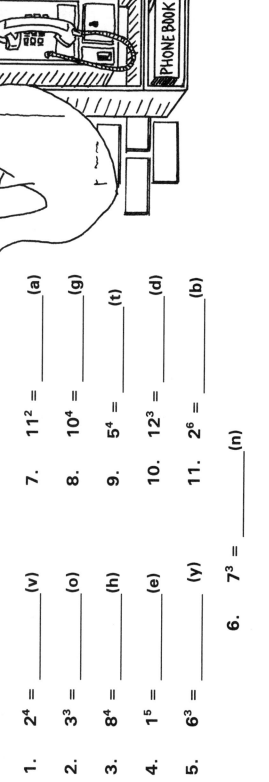
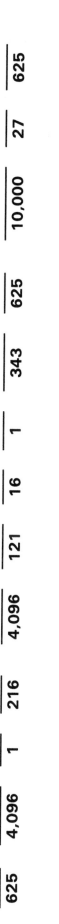

Decoder:

625 27 10,000 625 216

343 1,728 27 1 216 64 16 121 216 4,096 343

121 1 216 4,096 121 625

Multiplying powers

NAME_____

When do you learn to ride a camel?

DIRECTIONS: Find each product. Then locate your answer in the decoder. Each time your answer occurs in the decoder, write the letter of the problem above it.

1. $10^2 \times 10^3 =$ _____ (n)

2. $10^3 \times 10 \times 10^2 =$ _____ (v)

3. $(9b^3)(-3bc^3) =$ _____ (u)

4. $6wz^2 \cdot 7w^4z^3 =$ _____ (o)

5. $(3wz)(6w)(z^2) =$ _____ (a)

6. $b \cdot c \cdot c \cdot b \cdot c =$ _____ (t)

7. $(-w^2z)(6z^3)(-wz) =$ _____ (p)

8. $8^2 \cdot 5^2 \cdot 3^2 =$ _____ (r)

9. $2^4 \cdot 2^5 =$ _____ (w)

10. $b^3(b^5c^2) =$ _____ (e)

11. $w^6 \cdot w \cdot w^3 =$ _____ (m)

12. $(2z^2)(-2z^3)(-z) =$ _____ (h)

13. $5^3 \cdot 2^3 =$ _____ (y)

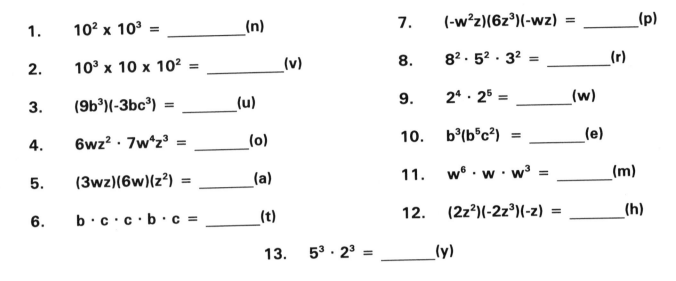

$\overline{}$ $\overline{}$ $\overline{}$ $\overline{}$
512    $4z^6$ b^8c^2 100,000

$\overline{}$ $\overline{}$ $\overline{}$
1000 $42w^5z^5$ $-27b^4c^3$

$\overline{}$ $\overline{}$ $\overline{}$
$18w^2z^3$ 14,400 b^8c^2

$\overline{}$ $\overline{}$ $\overline{}$ $\overline{}$
$42w^5z^5$ 1,000,000 b^8c^2 14,400

$\overline{}$ $\overline{}$ $\overline{}$
b^2c^3 $4z^6$ b^8c^2

$\overline{}$ $\overline{}$ $\overline{}$ $\overline{}$
$4z^6$ $-27b^4c^3$ w^{10} $6w^3z^5$

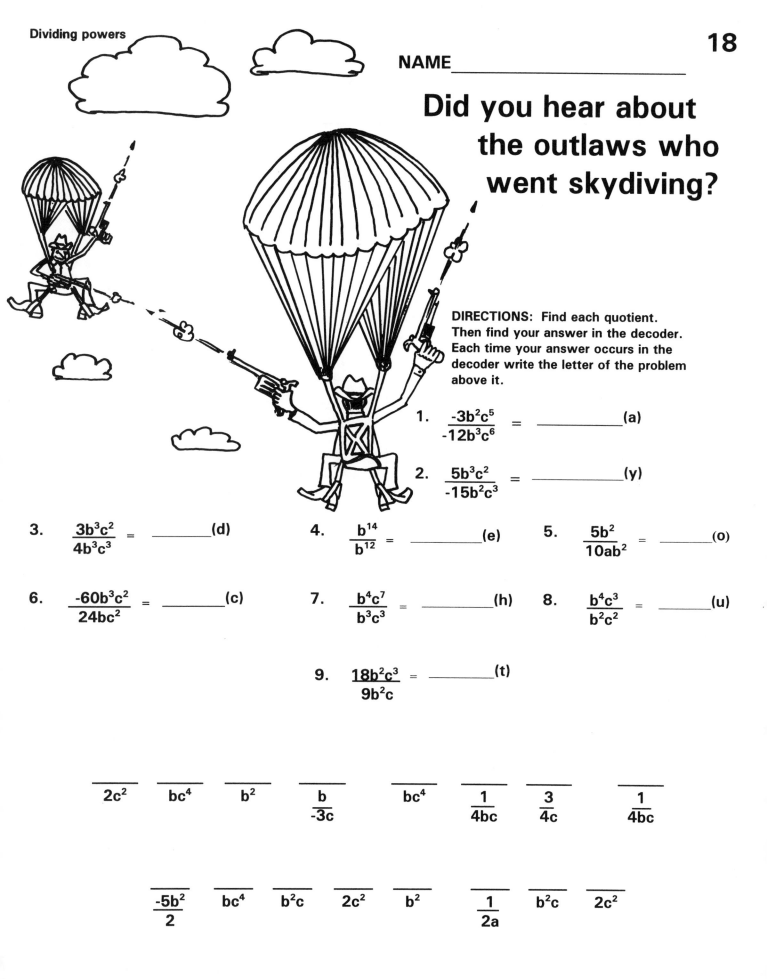

NAME_____

Did you hear about the outlaws who went skydiving?

DIRECTIONS: Find each quotient. Then find your answer in the decoder. Each time your answer occurs in the decoder write the letter of the problem above it.

1. $\dfrac{-3b^2c^5}{-12b^3c^6}$ = _____ (a)

2. $\dfrac{5b^3c^2}{-15b^2c^3}$ = _____ (y)

3. $\dfrac{3b^3c^2}{4b^3c^3}$ = _____ (d)

4. $\dfrac{b^{14}}{b^{12}}$ = _____ (e)

5. $\dfrac{5b^2}{10ab^2}$ = _____ (o)

6. $\dfrac{-60b^3c^2}{24bc^2}$ = _____ (c)

7. $\dfrac{b^4c^7}{b^3c^3}$ = _____ (h)

8. $\dfrac{b^4c^3}{b^2c^2}$ = _____ (u)

9. $\dfrac{18b^2c^3}{9b^2c}$ = _____ (t)

| $2c^2$ | bc^4 | b^2 | $\dfrac{b}{-3c}$ | bc^4 | $\dfrac{1}{4bc}$ | $\dfrac{3}{4c}$ | $\dfrac{1}{4bc}$ |

| $\dfrac{-5b^2}{2}$ | bc^4 | b^2c | $2c^2$ | b^2 | $\dfrac{1}{2a}$ | b^2c | $2c^2$ |

Determining numbers as prime or composite

COMPOSITE OR PRIME?

A **prime number** is a whole number *greater than one* that has *exactly two factors*, 1 and itself.

A **composite number** is a whole number *greater than one* that has more than two factors.

DIRECTIONS: Complete the table below. If the number is a composite, you will need to give only one set of factors to prove that the number is a composite. (For example, if the number is 24, you can give 6 and 4, or 12 and 2, or 8 and 3, but you need to only give one set.)

	Number	Factors	Composite or Prime?
1.	60	5,12	Composite
2.	9		
3.	27		
4.	33		
5.	2		
6.	37		
7.	63		
8.	73		
9.	87		
10.	89		

	Number	Factors	Composite or Prime?
11.	93		
12.	97		
13.	103		
14.	141		
15.	167		
16.	121		
17.	147		
18.	149		
19.	171		
20.	207		

Helpful Hint: You should have 8 prime numbers and 12 composite numbers!

Prime Factorization

DIRECTIONS: Using a factor tree, find the prime factorization of each number or monomial. Two examples have been done for you.

Factor -141 completely.

$$-141 = -1 \cdot 141$$
$$\quad | \quad /\backslash$$
$$-1 \cdot 3 \cdot 47$$
$$-141 = -1 \cdot 3 \cdot 47$$
(3 factors)

Factor 21 xy²

$$21xy^2 = 3 \cdot 7 \cdot x \cdot y^2$$
$$\quad | \quad | \quad | \quad /\backslash$$
$$3 \cdot 7 \cdot x \cdot y \cdot y$$
$$21xy^2 = 3 \cdot 7 \cdot x \cdot y \cdot y$$
(5 factors)

1. -110

(4 factors)

2. $143r^2s$

(5 factors)

3. -144

(7 factors)

4. $-16t^2s^2$

(9 factors)

5. $500bc^2$

(8 factors)

6. -140

(5 factors)

Use any method you choose to complete the prime factorization of each number or monomial.

7. $51j^2k$ _____ (5 factors)

8. $-625a^2b^2$ _____ (9 factors)

9. 98 _____ (3 factors)

10. $-1,600g^2$ _____ (11 factors)

11. 1521 _____ (4 factors)

12. $10,000$ _____ (8 factors)

NAME_____

What did the bald man say when he got a comb for his birthday?

DIRECTIONS: Find the greatest common factor for each of the problems. Then find your answer in the decoder. Each time your answer occurs in the decoder write the letter of the problem above it.

1. 25, 27 = _____(w)

2. $18xy$, $13x^2z$ = _____(h)

3. 40, 60, 120 = _____(s)

4. $-120x^2$, $150xy$ = _____(v)

5. 5, 10, 25 = _____(n)

6. $-5z^2$, $10z$, $15z^3$ = _____(l)

7. -60, 36 = _____(i)

8. $9b$, $30bc$, $42c$ = _____(k)

9. 32, 48, 80 = _____(e)

10. $12op^2$, $18o^3p$ = _____(t)

11. 36, 72 = _____(r)

12. $14d$, $21jf$, 35 = _____(a)

13. 33, 99, 198 = _____(p)

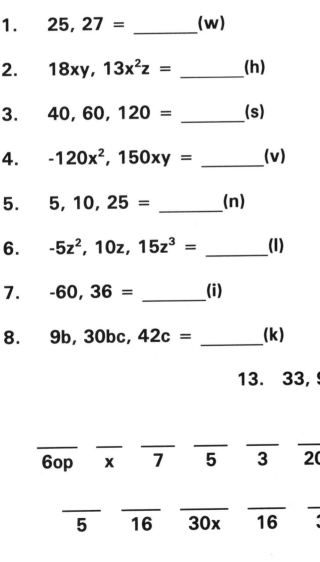

6op	x	7	5	3	20	12	1	12	5z	5z

5	16	30x	16	36	33	7	36	6op

1	12	6op	x	6op	x	12	20

NAME

Why are dogs seldom asked to play the piano?

Least common multiple

DIRECTIONS: Use prime factorization to find the least common multiple in each of the problems. Then find your answer in the decoder. Each time your answer occurs in the decoder write the letter of the problem above it.

1. 5, 7 = _____ (s)

2. 15k, 60k = _____ (n)

3. 4, 18 = _____ (o)

4. 5p, 15p², 30 = _____ (i)

5. 12p², 20 = _____ (w)

6. 27, 36 = _____ (h)

7. 15j, 35j² = _____ (e)

8. 8j, 12j, 16j = _____ (a)

9. 17, 51 = _____ (t)

10. 12k², 28 = _____ (r)

11. 25, 20 = _____ (c)

12. 6k, 30k, 24k² = _____ (b)

_____ _____ _____ _____ _____ _____ _____ _____ _____ _____
51 108 105j² 30p² 84k² 48j 120k² 100 108 108

_____ _____ _____ _____ _____ _____ _____ _____ _____ _____
60p² 108 36 84k² 35 105j² 51 108 51 30p² 48j 60k

_____ _____ _____ _____ _____ _____ _____
108 105j² 30p² 84k² 30p² 120k² 30p² 51 105j²

_____
51 35

© 1996 by Incentive Publications, Inc., Nashville, TN.

The Slide Method for GCF and LCM

DIRECTIONS: Examine the method shown below for finding the *greatest common factor, least common multiple,* and the *fraction in simplest form.*

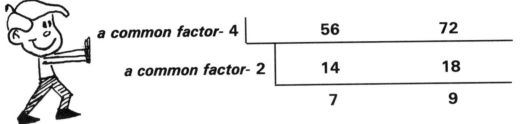

a common factor- 4	56	72
a common factor- 2	14	18
	7	9

A) To find the *GCF,* multiply the number outside the steps of the slide on the left side of the table: (4 x 2 = 8). (B) To find the *LCM,* multiply all of the numbers outside of the step of the slide's border and bottom of the slide: (4 x 2 x 7 x 9 = 504). (C) The fraction $\frac{56}{72}$ will be shown in simplest form by the two numbers underneath the slide. Therefore, the fraction is $\frac{7}{9}$ is in simplest form.

		GCF	LCM	Simplest form
1.	15, 30			
2.	24, 36			
3.	40, 62			
4.	12, 18			
5.	54, 72			
6.	64, 120			
7.	42, 112			
8.	64, 152			
9.	24, 56			

		GCF	LCM	Simplest form
10.	12, 15			
11.	20, 36			
12.	12, 16			
13.	15, 25			
14.	20, 32			
15.	18, 27			
16.	30, 80			
17.	33, 44			
18.	12, 20			

ANIMAL OLYMPICS

DIRECTIONS: To find the name of each animal, solve each problem. Find your answer in the decoder write the letter of the problem above it. Each time your answer occurs in the

Animal with the best tastebuds:

$\overline{37}$ $\overline{64}$ $\overline{72}$ $\overline{72}$ $\overline{97}$ $\overline{2}$ $\overline{96}$ $\overline{5}$ $\overline{18}$

Mammal that produces the most
young in a year:

$\overline{37}$ $\overline{2}$ $\overline{49}$ $\overline{12}$ $\overline{99}$ $\overline{2}$ $\overline{54}$ $\overline{72}$

Insect that can carry 850
times its own weight:

$\overline{2}$ $\overline{66}$ $\overline{60}$ $\overline{99}$ $\overline{49}$ $\overline{11}$ $\overline{97}$ $\overline{2}$ $\overline{49}$ $\overline{16}$ $\overline{37}$ $\overline{97}$ $\overline{97}$ $\overline{72}$ $\overline{5}$ $\overline{97}$

The largest snake which can
reach lengths of 19 ft or more

$\overline{54}$ $\overline{99}$ $\overline{54}$ $\overline{11}$ $\overline{49}$ $\overline{99}$ $\overline{29}$ $\overline{54}$ $\overline{72}$

1. Name a prime number between 25-30. ____ (d)

2. Name the GCF of 32 and 48. ____ (s)

3. Name the largest two digit multiple of 9. ____ (n)

4. Name the largest composite number between 1 and 50. ____ (o)

5. Name the LCM of 15 and 20. ____ (i)

6. Name the only even prime. ____ (r)

7. Name a 2 digit factor of 24 that is also a factor of 36. ____ (w)

8. Name a 2 digit multiple of 11 whose digits add up to 12. ____ (h)

9. Name the largest prime between 80 and 100. ____ (e)

10. Name the LCM of 9, 18, 27. ____ (a)

11. Name a two digit prime number that is a factor of 33. ____ (c)

12. Name a prime number that is a factor of 10 and 15. ____ (l)

13. Name the smallest even number divisible by 6 and 9. ____ (y)

14. Name the LCM of 24 and 36. ____ (t)

15. Name the largest 2 digit multiple of 8. ____ (f)

16. Name the GCF of 37 and 74. ____ (b)

17. Name the 2 digit multiple of 8 whose digits add up to 10. ____ (u)

Simplifying fractions

What did one mountain say to the other mountain after the earthquake?

NAME _____

DIRECTIONS: Write each fraction in simplest form. Find your answer in the decoder. Each time your answer occurs in the decoder write the letter of the problem above it.

1. $\dfrac{6}{8}$ = _____ (s)

2. $\dfrac{27}{33}$ = _____ (i)

3. $\dfrac{16}{32}$ = _____ (m)

4. $\dfrac{30}{35}$ = _____ (n)

5. $\dfrac{15tv^2}{50tv}$ = _____ (o)

6. $\dfrac{12a^2b^2}{20ab^2}$ = _____ (a)

7. $\dfrac{16}{24}$ = _____ (y)

8. $\dfrac{14fg}{21f}$ = _____ (u)

9. $\dfrac{33}{77}$ = _____ (t)

10. $\dfrac{16r^2s^2}{2r^3s}$ = _____ (f)

11. $\dfrac{32m^3n}{42m^2n^2}$ = _____ (l)

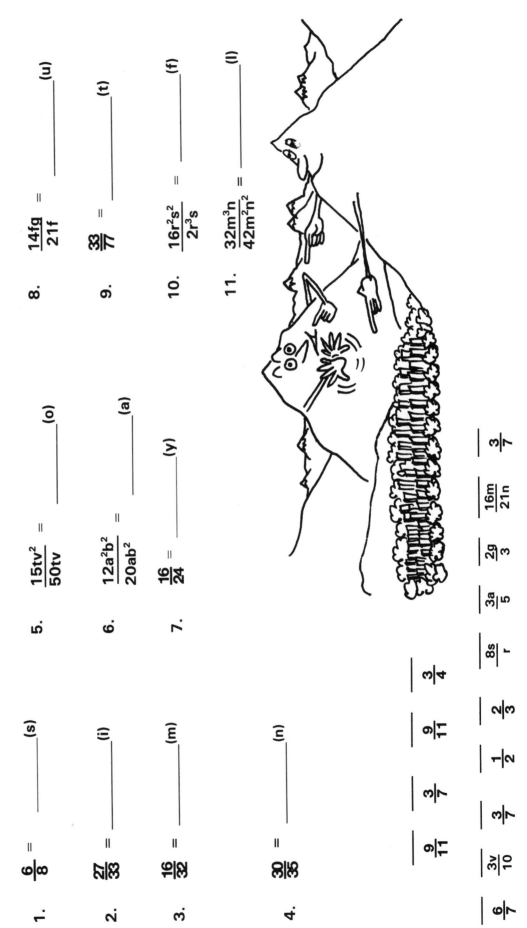

Decoder:

$\dfrac{6}{7}$ _____ $\dfrac{3v}{10}$ _____ $\dfrac{9}{11}$ _____ $\dfrac{3}{7}$ _____ $\dfrac{1}{2}$ _____ $\dfrac{3}{7}$ _____ $\dfrac{2}{3}$ _____ $\dfrac{9}{11}$ _____ $\dfrac{3}{4}$ _____ $\dfrac{8s}{r}$ _____ $\dfrac{3a}{5}$ _____ $\dfrac{2g}{3}$ _____ $\dfrac{16m}{21n}$ _____ $\dfrac{3}{7}$

Writing decimals as fractions

What is the laziest mountain?

DIRECTIONS: Express each decimal as a fraction or mixed number in simplest terms. Find your answer in the decoder. Each time your answer occurs in the decoder write the letter of the problem above it.

1. $0.6 =$ _____ (o)

2. $-0.\overline{072} =$ _____ (m)

3. $0.\overline{45} =$ _____ (u)

4. $-0.95 =$ _____ (n)

5. $5.75 =$ _____ (s)

6. $0.432 =$ _____ (t)

7. $0.1 =$ _____ (v)

8. $-0.\overline{96} =$ _____ (e)

9. $0.8 =$ _____ (r)

$-\frac{32}{33}$ $-\frac{8}{111}$ $\frac{3}{5}$ $\frac{5}{11}$ $-\frac{19}{20}$ $\frac{54}{125}$

$\frac{1}{10}$ $-\frac{32}{33}$ $\frac{4}{5}$ $-\frac{32}{33}$ $5\frac{3}{4}$ $\frac{54}{125}$

NAME _____

Why did the lumberjack give away his firewood?

DIRECTIONS: Solve each problem and then find your answer in the decoder. Each time your answer occurs, write the letter of the problem above it.

Round to the nearest tenth:

1. 54.317 = _____ (o)

2. 54.396 = _____ (g)

3. 81.95 = _____ (t)

4. 64.0975 = _____ (s)

Round to the nearest hundredth:

5. 64.189 = _____ (n)

6. 81.139 = _____ (i)

7. 81.241 = _____ (h)

8. 7,016.319 = _____ (e)

Round to the nearest thousandth:

9. 971.5405 = _____ (f)

10. 971.6934 = _____ (a)

11. 2.1984 = _____ (w)

12. 2.9815 = _____ (x)

13. 54.4938 = _____ (r)

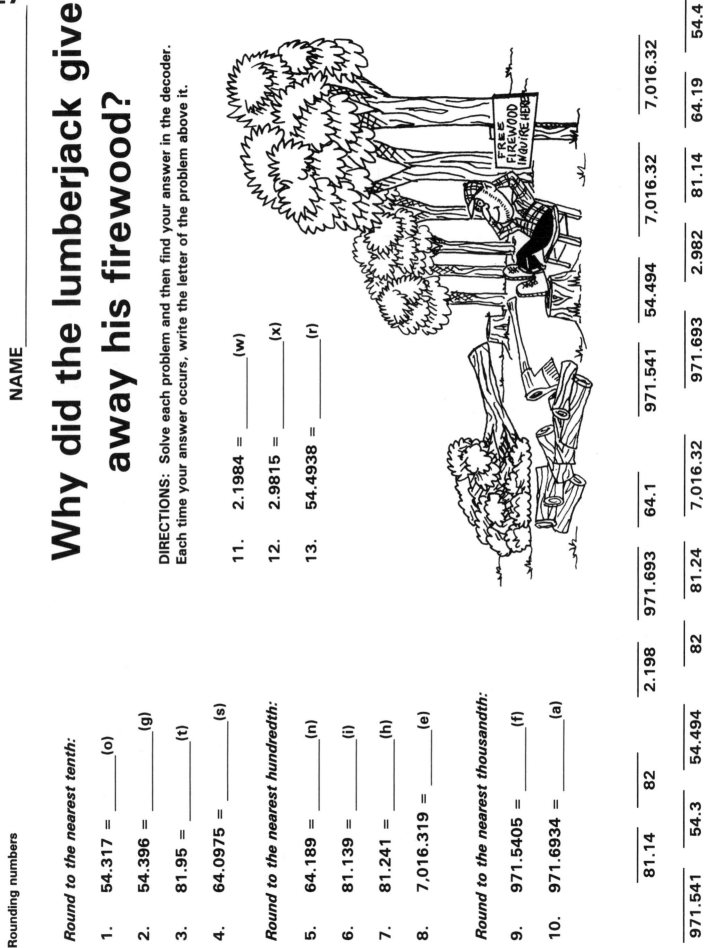

| 971.541 | 54.3 | 82 | 54.494 | 81.14 | 82 | 2.198 | 971.693 | 64.1 | 7,016.32 | 971.693 | 971.541 | 54.494 | 7,016.32 | 7,016.32 | 64.19 | 54.4 |
| 81.24 | 2.982 | 81.14 |

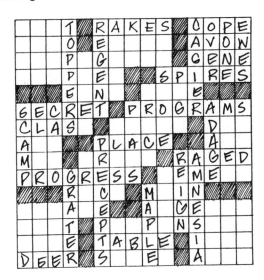

Why is a crossword puzzle like an argument?

DIRECTIONS: Estimate each sum and difference to the nearest whole number. Find your answer in the decoder. Each time your answer occurs in the decoder, write the letter of the problem above it.

1.   736.4 + 13.9 = _____ (e)

2.   15.73 - 1.897 = _____ (t)

3.   8.435 + 6.71 + 32.2 = _____ (n)

4.   28.3 - 3.628 = _____ (a)

5.   0.752 + 0.9 + 0.22 = _____ (s)

6.   16.61 - 1.69 = _____ (r)

7.   8.4 + 3.9 + 6.24 = _____ (h)

8.   36.82 - 1.34 = _____ (o)

9.   27.9 + .93 + 2.98 = _____ (d)

10.   17.34 - 8.12 = _____ (l)

11.   6.724 + 3.219 + 0.542 = _____ (w)

| 36 | 47 | 750 | 11 | 36 | 15 | 32 |

| 9 | 750 | 24 | 32 | 2 |

| 14 | 36 |

| 24 | 47 | 36 | 14 | 18 | 750 | 15 |

What is a volcano?

NAME _____

Adding and subtracting decimals

DIRECTIONS: Solve each problem. Find your answer in the decoder. Each time your answer occurs in the decoder write the letter of the problem above it.

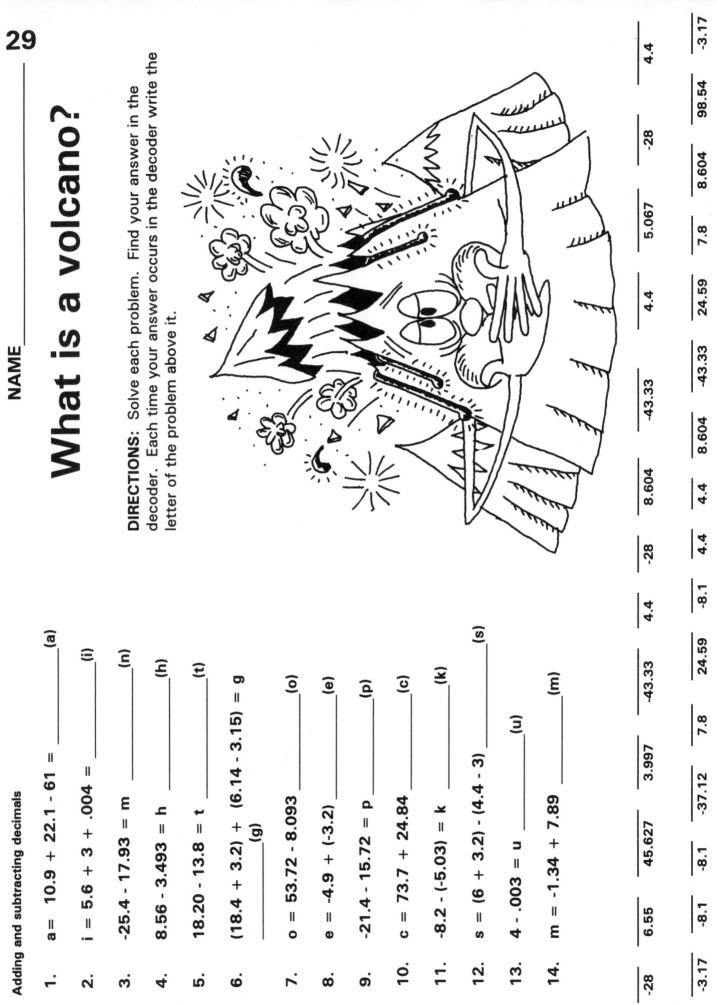

1. $a = 10.9 + 22.1 - 61 =$ _____ (a)

2. $i = 5.6 + 3 + .004 =$ _____ (i)

3. $-25.4 - 17.93 = m$ _____ (n)

4. $8.56 - 3.493 = h$ _____ (h)

5. $18.20 - 13.8 = t$ _____ (t)

6. $(18.4 + 3.2) + (6.14 - 3.15) = g$ _____ (g)

7. $o = 53.72 - 8.093$ _____ (o)

8. $e = -4.9 + (-3.2)$ _____ (e)

9. $-21.4 - 15.72 = p$ _____ (p)

10. $c = 73.7 + 24.84$ _____ (c)

11. $-8.2 - (-5.03) = k$ _____ (k)

12. $s = (6 + 3.2) - (4.4 - 3)$ _____ (s)

13. $4 - .003 = u$ _____ (u)

14. $m = -1.34 + 7.89$ _____ (m)

Decoder:

-3.17	-28	6.55	45.627	-8.1	-37.12	3.997	-43.33	7.8	24.59	4.4	-8.1	4.4	-28	8.604	4.4	-43.33	8.604	4.4	24.59	5.067	8.604	-28	98.54	4.4
-8.1	45.627	-37.12	7.8	-8.1		7.8																	-3.17	

Does your checkbook balance?

Directions: *In order to keep an accurate account of the amount of money you have in the bank, you need to keep your checkbook register up-to-date and balanced. In this register you record all your transactions and then calculate your new balance.*

- 1.   *Record check number and date.*
- 2.   *Record to whom the check was made.*
- 3.   *Write the amount of the check.*
- 4.   *Subtract each check amount from the last balance.*
- 5.   *Add each deposit amount to the last balance.*

Use your calculator to complete the check register shown here. Be sure to show the new balance after each check or deposit. You will be filling in only the "BALANCE" column. The first two have been done for you.

DATE	CHECK NUMBER	DESCRIPTION OF TRANSACTION	PAYMENT (-)	✓ T	DEPOSIT AMOUNT	BALANCE
						$396.40
3/15	204	Bob's Grocery	$54.36			$342.04
3/16	205	Jock's Fitness Center	$45.00			$297.04
3/17		DEPOSIT			$150.75	_____
3/17	206	Car Payment	$190.75			_____
3/18	207	Theater Tickets	$50.00			_____
3/19		DEPOSIT			$210.80	_____
3/21	208	Roy's Mountain Bike Shop	$59.65			_____
3/22	209	Car Insurance	$210.85			_____
3/23		DEPOSIT			$470.00	_____

NAME_____

Why did the nasty kid put ice cubes in his aunt's bed?

DIRECTIONS: Solve each problem. Find your answer in the decoder. Each time your answer occurs in the decoder, write the letter of the problem above it.

1. 6 tons = _____ lb (d)

2. 365 days = _____ yr (w)

3. 3,000 lb = _____ ton (h)

4. 104 pt = _____ gal (r)

5. 6 qt = _____ pt (o)

6. 10,560 ft = _____ mi (e)

7. 1 mi = _____ yd (n)

8. 2 ft 3 in
   + 5 ft 11 in
   _____ = (t)

9. 9 gal 1 qt
   - 3 gal 3 qt
   _____ = (f)

10. 4 yd 2 ft
    + 3 yd 2 ft
    _____ = (z)

11. 6 ft 11 in
    + 1 ft 4 in
    _____ = (i)

12. 3 gal
    - 1 gal 2 qt
    _____ = (a)

13. 6 gal
    -    8 qts.
    _____ = (s)

1.5	2	1	1 gal 2 qt	1,760	8 ft 2 in	2	12,000	8 ft 2 in	12	4 gal	2	2

	1 gal 2 qt	1,760	8 ft 2 in	8 ft 3 in	5 gal 2 qt	13	2	2	8 yd 1 ft	2

If a father gave his daughter 15¢ and his son 10¢, what time is it?

DIRECTIONS: Express each fraction as a decimal. Use a bar to show a repeating decimal. Use a calculator when necessary.

1. $\frac{5}{6}$ = _____ (u)

2. $\frac{19}{25}$ = _____ (a)

3. $2\frac{7}{8}$ = _____ (e)

4. $1\frac{11}{12}$ = _____ (r)

5. $\frac{5}{12}$ = _____ (o)

6. $\frac{7}{16}$ = _____ (w)

7. $\frac{7}{33}$ = _____ (q)

8. $\frac{3}{5}$ = _____ (t)

| $\overline{0.76}$ | $0.\overline{21}$ | $0.8\overline{3}$ | $\overline{0.76}$ | $1.91\overline{6}$ | $\overline{0.6}$ | $\overline{2.875}$ | $1.91\overline{6}$ |

| | $\overline{0.6}$ | $0.41\overline{6}$ | | $\overline{0.6}$ | $\overline{0.4375}$ | $0.41\overline{6}$ |

NAME _____

Why is it difficult to eat soup with a moustache?

DIRECTIONS: Solve each equation. Find your answer in the decoder. Each time your answer occurs in the decoder write the letter of the problem above it.

1. $(0.32)(-1.4) = a$ $(a = \underline{\quad})$

2. $-7(4.3) = c$ $(c = \underline{\quad})$

3. $i = 10(-16.81)$ $(i = \underline{\quad})$

4. $e = (8.003)(0.3)$ $(e = \underline{\quad})$

5. $s = (-6.5)(-8.62)$ $(s = \underline{\quad})$

6. $40(8.2) = b$ $(b = \underline{\quad})$

7. $n = (-5.03)(-3.6)$ $(n = \underline{\quad})$

8. $(118.91)(-2) = u$ $(u = \underline{\quad})$

9. $(21.9)(6) = t$ $(t = \underline{\quad})$

10. $(-7.3)(1.006) = r$ $(r = \underline{\quad})$

11. $q = (-4)(-8.46)$ $(q = \underline{\quad})$

Decoder (top):
56.03 -168.1 -0.448 131.4 -7.3438 -168.1 2.4009 56.03 18.108

Decoder (bottom):
328 2.4009 -237.82 -30.1 -0.448 -168.1 131.4 2.4009 -237.82 56.03 -168.1 33.84

NAME_____

What kind of special rates do parrot hotels offer?

DIRECTIONS: Solve each equation. Find your answer in the decoder. Each time your answer occurs in the decoder write the letter of the problem above it.

1. $3.066 \div 0.3 = y$ $(y = \underline{\hspace{1cm}})$

2. $e = 3.66 \div 0.061$ $(e = \underline{\hspace{1cm}})$

3. $-4.03 \div (-62) = h$ $(h = \underline{\hspace{1cm}})$

4. $f = -.0432 \div (-.012)$ $(f = \underline{\hspace{1cm}})$

5. $30.91 \div 11 = p$ $(p = \underline{\hspace{1cm}})$

6. $3.75 \div (-0.5) = i$ $(i = \underline{\hspace{1cm}})$

7. $22.375 \div 8.95 = t$ $(t = \underline{\hspace{1cm}})$

8. $0.2895 \div 0.5 = a$ $(a = \underline{\hspace{1cm}})$

9. $-0.672 \div (-67.2) = o$ $(o = \underline{\hspace{1cm}})$

10. $u = 40.05 \div (-4.5)$ $(u = \underline{\hspace{1cm}})$

11. $-4.045 \div 0.005 = n$ $(n = \underline{\hspace{1cm}})$

12. $135 \div 15 = s$ $(s = \underline{\hspace{1cm}})$

13. $5.44 \div (-17) = c$ $(c = \underline{\hspace{1cm}})$

14. $1.0759 \div (-2.03) = r$ $(r = \underline{\hspace{1cm}})$

| 2.5 | 0.01 | -8.9 | -0.32 | 0.579 | -809 | | 9 | 2.5 | 0.579 | 10.22 |

| 3.6 | 0.01 | -0.53 | 2.5 | 0.065 | 60 | 2.81 | -0.53 | -7.5 | -0.32 | 60 |

| 0.01 | 3.6 | | 0.01 | -809 | 60 |

© 1996 by Incentive Publications, Inc., Nashville, TN.

NAME _____

GAS MILEAGE RATE(MPG)

Do you know how many miles your family can drive on one gallon of gas? To figure a car's gas mileage rate(MPG), use this
formula: (Miles driven ÷ Gallons used = Miles per gallon) Use your calculator to complete Tim's mileage record starting
with the September 10 fill-up. Round your answers to the nearest tenth. The first one has been done for you.

	ODOMETER READINGS			GASOLINE USED	
Date Car was filled up	The odometer reading when filled up	−	The last odometer reading	=	Miles driven	÷	Gallons used	=	Miles per gallon
Sept. 10	8,728.0	8,375.4	352.6	11.3	31.2
Sept. 18	9,075.4	8,728.0	347.4	11.2	
Sept. 27	9,374.1	9,075.4	298.7	10.8	
Oct. 3	9,616	9,374.1	241.9	8.7	
Oct. 10	9,974.9	9,616	358.9	11.5	

Interpreting the Data

1.   The average of the five MPGs is _____.

2.   What might account for the differences in the MPGs? _____

_____

Extension Activity: *Make a chart similar to this one for one of your family's cars for a month. Calculate your MPG.*

Using a calculator to determine batting averages

WHAT'S THE BATTING AVERAGE?

DIRECTIONS: To find a batting average, divide the number of hits by the number of times at bat. Drop the zero before the decimal point and round to the nearest thousandth.
Example: Katie has 37 hits with 95 times at bat. 37 ÷ 95 = 0.389473684 (Rounded to .389) Katie's batting average is .389.

DIRECTIONS: Complete the table to find these batting averages.

	Player	Hits ÷	Times at bat	= Batting Average
a.	Paul	25	60	
b.	Reid	52	78	
c.	Sarah	33	90	

Now, for the big leagues! Listed below are the 10 leading batters for two professional baseball leagues. Use your calculator and determine these batting averages.

MAJOR LEAGUE BATTING LEADERS

PLAYER	TEAM	LEAGUE	AT BAT(AB)	HITS(H)	BATTING AVERAGE
Hutchinson	San Diego	League A	419	165	
Gower	Houston	League A	400	147	
Horsman	New York	League B	368	132	
Norton	Cleveland	League B	412	147	
Florentine	Chicago	League B	399	141	
Syrios	Cleveland	League B	459	160	
Leiner	New York	League B	366	125	
Swigart	Montreal	League A	422	143	
Callner	Cincinnati	League A	436	146	
Sapitowicz	Cincinnati	League A	310	101	

1. Which teams had the most representatives on this list? _____

2. Which league, A or B, had the greatest combined average of its top five hitters? _____
How much greater was the average? _____

Using scientific notation

Why are the buffalo having a parade?

DIRECTIONS: Solve each equation below. Then find your answer in the decoder. Each time your answer occurs, write the letter of the problem above it.

1. $7.3 \times 10^3 =$ _____ (r)

2. $9.643 \times 10^4 =$ _____ (i)

3. $-3.16 \times 10^{-5} =$ _____ (h)

4. $-2.104 \times 10^0 =$ _____ (o)

5. $-3.11 \times 10^5 =$ _____ (y)

6. $-1.3694 \times 10^1 =$ _____ (n)

7. $7.08 \times 10^{-4} =$ _____ (s)

8. $4.7 \times 10^4 =$ _____ (t)

9. $8.94 \times 10^{11} =$ _____ (g)

10. $3.4 \times 10^2 =$ _____ (e)

11. $3.11 \times 10^4 =$ _____ (b)

12. $-7.3 \times 10^{-2} =$ _____ (a)

13. $1.3694 \times 10^2 =$ _____ (l)

14. $-80 \times 10^0 =$ _____ (c)

_____ _____ _____ _____ _____ _____
47,000 -0.0000316 7,300 136.94 340

_____ _____ _____ _____ _____
-311,000 340 340 31,100 340

894,000,000,000 -13.694 96,430 47,000 -0.073 7,300

-0.073 -80

NAME_____

Why do mummies never tell secrets?

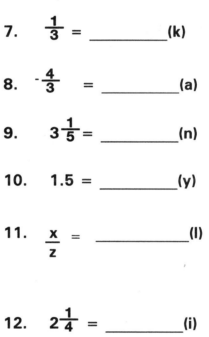

DIRECTIONS: Solve each equation. Find your answer in the decoder. Each time your answer occurs in the decoder write the letter of the problem above it.

Multiply these fractions:

1. $\frac{1}{7} \cdot \frac{1}{7} =$ _____ (u)

2. $-3\frac{1}{3} \cdot 1\frac{3}{5} =$ _____ (h)

3. $(1\frac{1}{9})(\frac{17}{30}) =$ _____ (g)

4. $3(\frac{3}{5})^2 =$ _____ (s)

5. $(\frac{1}{2})^2 =$ _____ (o)

6. A peregrine falcon flies at speeds up to 225 mph. A golden eagle flies about two-thirds as fast. How fast does the golden eagle fly? _____ (r)

Name the multiplication inverse of each rational number:

7. $\frac{1}{3} =$ _____ (k)

8. $\frac{-4}{3} =$ _____ (a)

9. $3\frac{1}{5} =$ _____ (n)

10. $1.5 =$ _____ (y)

11. $\frac{x}{z} =$ _____ (l)

12. $2\frac{1}{4} =$ _____ (i)

Divide these fractions:

13. $-10 \div \frac{3}{2} =$ _____ (p)

14. How many boards each 2 ft 4 in. long can be cut from a board 12 ft long? = _____ (e)

15. $4 \div \frac{1}{2} =$ _____ (d)

16. $\frac{5}{8} \div (-2) =$ _____ (t)

17. Lindsay had 6¼ cups of flour on hand to use for cakes she wants to make for the school sale. If the recipe calls for 1½ cups of flour, how many cakes can she make? _____ (w)

| $-\frac{5}{16}$ | $-5\frac{1}{3}$ | 5 | $\frac{2}{3}$ | $\frac{z}{x}$ | $\frac{4}{9}$ | 3 | 5 | $-\frac{5}{16}$ | $\frac{1}{4}$ | 3 | 5 | 5 | $-6\frac{2}{3}$ |

| $-\frac{5}{16}$ | $-5\frac{1}{3}$ | $\frac{4}{9}$ | $\frac{5}{16}$ | $\frac{17}{27}$ | $12\frac{24}{25}$ | $\frac{1}{49}$ | $\frac{5}{16}$ | 8 | 5 | 150 | 4 | 150 | $-\frac{3}{4}$ | $-6\frac{2}{3}$ | $12\frac{24}{25}$ |

NAME_____

Can you decipher this message?

I O O 4 I 8 O

DIRECTIONS: Solve each equation. Find your answer in the decoder. Each time your answer occurs in the decoder write the letter of the problem above it.

1. $3g + 11 = 26$ (g = _____)

2. $4 - 5f = 64$ (f = _____)

3. $6 - 5r = -94$ (r = _____)

4. $24 = \dfrac{h}{18 - 16} - 14$ (h = _____)

5. $44 = 8t + (-4)$ (t = _____)

6. $-10 = \dfrac{a + 3}{3}$ (a = _____)

7. $16 = 7 - w$ (w = _____)

8. $-12 + \dfrac{e}{6 + 0} = 0$ (e = _____)

9. $6o - 12 = 36$ (o = _____)

10. $\dfrac{n}{16} = -30$ (n = _____)

11. $\dfrac{i}{12} - 15 = 31$ (i = _____)

| 552 | 8 | -9 | 72 | -480 | 8 | 6 | -288 | 552 | -480 | 5 |

| -12 | 8 | 20 | 552 | -33 | 6 | 72 |

| -480 | 8 | 6 | -288 | 552 | -480 | 5 |

What is a sound sleeper?

DIRECTIONS: Define a variable and then write and solve the equation. Find your answer in the decoder. Each time your answer occurs in the decoder write the letter of the problem above it.

1. In one season, Ken scored 19 soccer goals. He scored three fewer goals than twice the number of goals scored by Paul. How many goals did Paul score? Let e = goals scored by Paul._____(e)

2. Find a number such that eight less than twice the number is 32. Let h = the number. _____(h)

3. Katie hit four more home runs than three times the number of home runs hit by Kristen. Together they hit 20 home runs. How many home runs did Kristen hit? Let o = home runs hit by Kristen. _____(o)

4. The cost of a sweater vest and a blouse is $57. The sweater vest cost twice as much as the blouse. Let r = the price of the blouse. What is the price of the blouse? _____(r)

5. Fourteen more than three times a number is -82. Let p = number. What is the number? _____(p)

6. Nathan bought a CD player for $30 more than one-half of the original price. If he paid $120 for the CD player, what was the original price? Let n = the original price. _____(n)

7. Twelve more than six times a number is 30. Find the number. Let s = the number. _____(s)

8. Twelve less than 2 times a number is 40. Let a = the number. _____(a)

9. Find a number such that ten more than three times the number is 52. Let w = the number. _____(w)

26	-32	11	19	3	4	180	14	20	4	3	180	4	19	11	3

NAME_____

What furniture polish do schools use?

DIRECTIONS: Solve each equation mentally. Find your answer in the decoder. Each time your answer occurs in the decoder write the letter of the problem above it.

1. $\dfrac{o}{8} = 4$ (o = _____)

2. $18 = n - 3$ (n = _____)

3. $24 = 16 + f$ (f = _____)

4. $\dfrac{g}{7} = 7$ (g = _____)

5. $6i = 90$ (i = _____)

6. $72 = 8p$ (p = _____)

7. $8 = 5l + 3$ (l = _____)

8. $30 = e + 12$ (e = _____)

9. $\dfrac{100}{d} = 10$ (d = _____)

10. $\dfrac{a}{8} = 0$ (a = _____)

11. $60 = c + 15$ (c = _____)

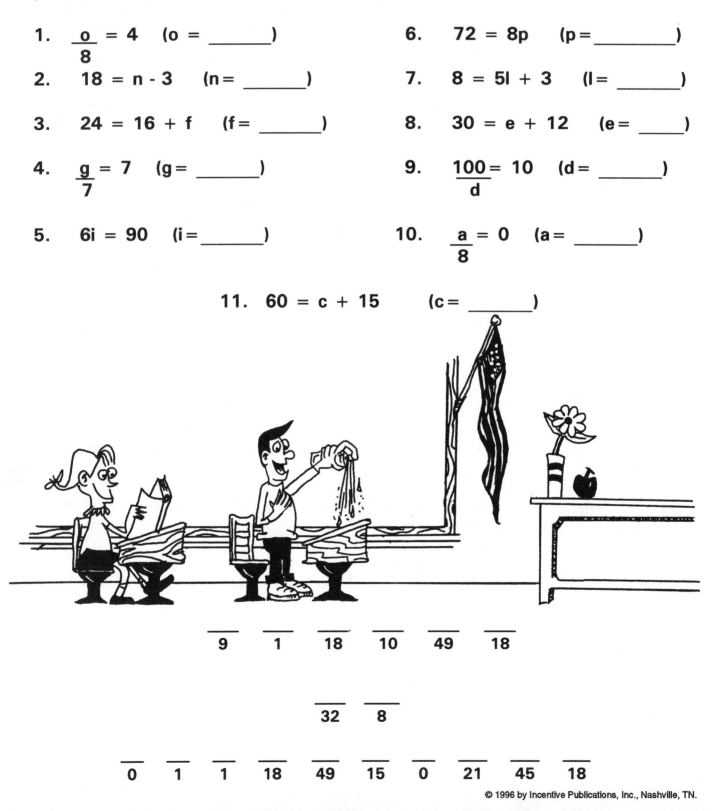

$\overline{9}$ $\overline{1}$ $\overline{18}$ $\overline{10}$ $\overline{49}$ $\overline{18}$

$\overline{32}$ $\overline{8}$

$\overline{0}$ $\overline{1}$ $\overline{1}$ $\overline{18}$ $\overline{49}$ $\overline{15}$ $\overline{0}$ $\overline{21}$ $\overline{45}$ $\overline{18}$

NAME _____

What did Noah say when the animals started climbing into the ark?

DIRECTIONS: Solve each equation. Find your answer in the decoder. Each time your answer occurs in the decoder write the letter of the problem above it.

1. $5v - 32 = 3v$ (v = _____)

2. $-33g + 58 = 98g - 73$ (g = _____)

3. $18w - 21 = 15w + 3$ (w = _____)

4. $6o - 12 = 2o + 36$ (o = _____)

5. $2y = 3y + 2$ (y = _____)

6. $7 + 6n = 8n - 13$ (n = _____)

7. $-53 - 2i = -i + 20$ (i = _____)

8. $1.6 - d = 12.8 + 3d$ (d = _____)

9. $6e = 3e - 15$ (e = _____)

10. $7r + 17 = 4r - 25$ (r = _____)

11. $-3h = 96 + 5h$ (h = _____)

12. $4t = 3t + 3$ (t = _____)

Decoder:

$\overline{}$ $\overline{}$ $\overline{}$ $\overline{}$ $\overline{}$ $\overline{}$ $\overline{}$ $\overline{}$
10   12   8   -73   -12   -5   -14   -2.8

$\overline{}$ $\overline{}$ $\overline{}$ $\overline{}$ $\overline{}$ $\overline{}$ $\overline{}$ $\overline{}$ $\overline{}$ $\overline{}$
-5   16   -5   -14   -2   3   -12   -73   10   1

NAME _____

Solving multi-step equations

Why did the student want to study oceanography?

DIRECTIONS: Solve each equation, and then find your answer in the decoder. Each time your answer occurs in the decoder, write the letter of the problem above it.

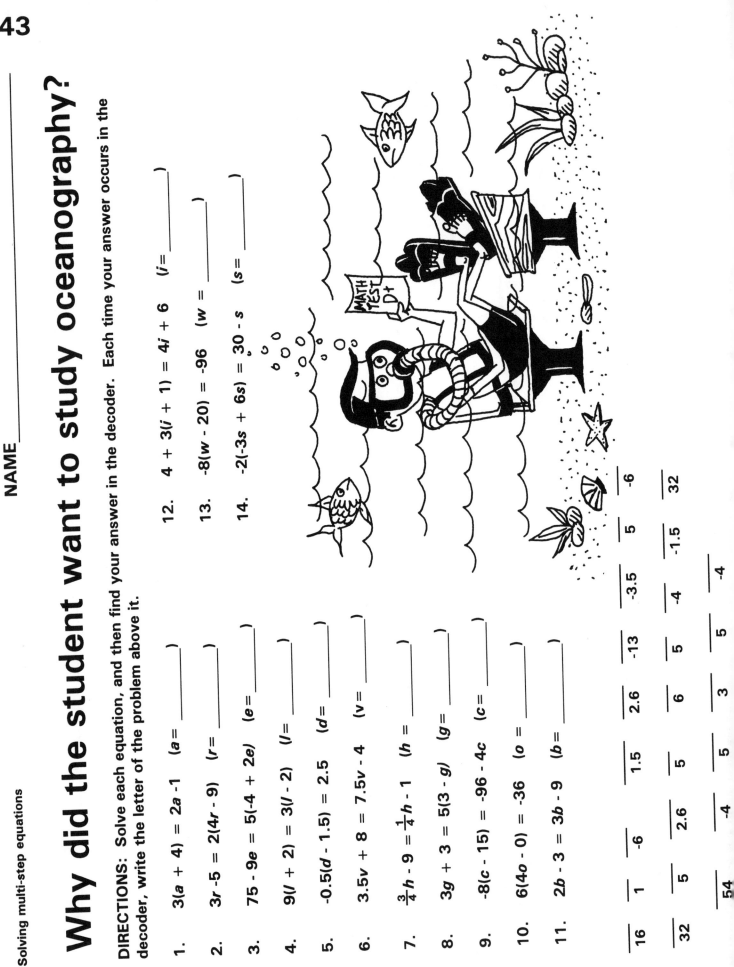

1. $3(a + 4) = 2a - 1$ $(a =$ _____ $)$

2. $3r - 5 = 2(4r - 9)$ $(r =$ _____ $)$

3. $75 - 9e = 5(-4 + 2e)$ $(e =$ _____ $)$

4. $9(l + 2) = 3(l - 2)$ $(l =$ _____ $)$

5. $-0.5(d - 1.5) = 2.5$ $(d =$ _____ $)$

6. $3.5v + 8 = 7.5v - 4$ $(v =$ _____ $)$

7. $\frac{3}{4}h - 9 = \frac{1}{4}h - 1$ $(h =$ _____ $)$

8. $3g + 3 = 5(3 - g)$ $(g =$ _____ $)$

9. $-8(c - 15) = -96 - 4c$ $(c =$ _____ $)$

10. $6(4o - 0) = -36$ $(o =$ _____ $)$

11. $2b - 3 = 3b - 9$ $(b =$ _____ $)$

12. $4 + 3(i + 1) = 4i + 6$ $(i =$ _____ $)$

13. $-8(w - 20) = -96$ $(w =$ _____ $)$

14. $-2(-3s + 6s) = 30 - s$ $(s =$ _____ $)$

$\overline{16}$	$\overline{1}$	$\overline{-6}$	$\overline{1.5}$	$\overline{2.6}$	$\overline{-13}$	$\overline{-3.5}$	$\overline{5}$	$\overline{-6}$
$\overline{32}$	$\overline{5}$	$\overline{2.6}$	$\overline{5}$	$\overline{6}$	$\overline{5}$	$\overline{-4}$	$\overline{-1.5}$	$\overline{32}$
$\overline{54}$	$\overline{-4}$	$\overline{5}$	$\overline{3}$	$\overline{5}$	$\overline{-4}$			

NAME _____

THE SEARCH IS ON!
(The Metric System)

DIRECTIONS: Look for many, varied and unusual objects that will fit in each category below.

Objects that weigh about 1 gram

1. _____

2. _____

Objects that weigh about 50 grams

1. _____

2. _____

Objects that weigh about 1 kilogram

1. _____

2. _____

Objects that will hold about 750 milliliters

1. _____

2. _____

Objects that will hold about 10 liters

1. _____

2. _____

Objects that measure about 10 centimeters

1. _____

2. _____

Objects that measure about 2 meters

1. _____

2. _____

Objects that measure about 1 - 5 millimeters

1. _____

2. _____

Objects that will hold about 10 milliliters of liquid

1. _____

2. _____

Objects that will hold about 1 liter

1. _____

2. _____

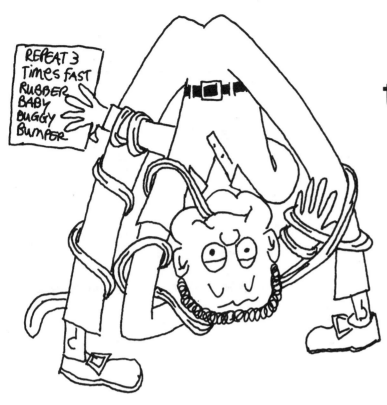

What is a tongue twister?

DIRECTIONS: Solve each equation, and then find your answer in the decoder. Each time your answer occurs in the decoder write the letter of the problem above it.

1. 3000 mm = _____m (y)

2. 2.9 kg = _____g (r)

3. 380 mL = _____L (e)

4. 3,821 m = _____km (w)

5. 0.002 kg = _____g (n)

6. 12 km = _____m (h)

7. 75 g = _____kg (o)

8. 4,000 mm = _____cm (a)

9. 0.02 m = _____mm (i)

10. 3,752 m = _____km (d)

11. 7,500 mg = _____kg (l)

12. 65 kg = _____g (s)

13. 382.1 mm = _____m (u)

14. .003752 km _____mm (g)

15. .038 L = _____mL (t)

20	38	20	65,000		3.821	12,000	0.38	2

	3	0.075	0.3821	2,900		38	400	2	3,752

3,752	0.38	38	65,000	38	0.075	0.3821	2	3,752	0.0075	0.38	3.752

Can you decode this old saying?

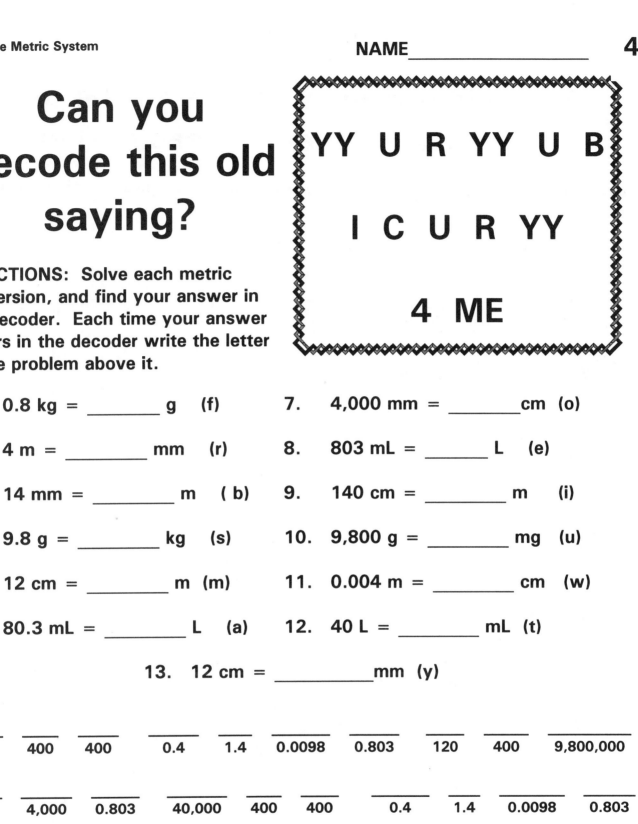

```
YY U R YY U B

  I C U R YY

    4 ME
```

DIRECTIONS: Solve each metric conversion, and find your answer in the decoder. Each time your answer occurs in the decoder write the letter of the problem above it.

1. 0.8 kg = _____ g (f)

2. 4 m = _____ mm (r)

3. 14 mm = _____ m (b)

4. 9.8 g = _____ kg (s)

5. 12 cm = _____ m (m)

6. 80.3 mL = _____ L (a)

7. 4,000 mm = _____cm (o)

8. 803 mL = _____ L (e)

9. 140 cm = _____ m (i)

10. 9,800 g = _____ mg (u)

11. 0.004 m = _____ cm (w)

12. 40 L = _____ mL (t)

13. 12 cm = _____mm (y)

40,000	400	400	0.4	1.4	0.0098	0.803	120	400	9,800,000

0.0803	4,000	0.803	40,000	400	400	0.4	1.4	0.0098	0.803

120	400	9,800,000	0.014	0.803	1.4	0.0098	0.803	0.803

120	400	9,800,000	0.0803	4,000	0.803	40,000	400	400

0.4	1.4	0.0098	0.803	800	400	4,000	0.12	0.803

What did one mummy say to the other mummy when they left each other?

DIRECTIONS: Solve each equation and graph your solution. Then find your answer in the decoder and write the letter of the problem above it.

1. $3n = -15$

    $n = \underline{\quad}$

2. $3g + 10 = -11$

    $g = \underline{\quad}$

3. $4y + 6 = 14$

    $y = \underline{\quad}$

4. $5o + 7 = 3o + 5$

    $o = \underline{\quad}$

| -7 | -6 | -5 | -4 | -3 | -2 | -1 | 0 | 1 | 2 |

| -7 | -6 | -5 | -4 | -3 | -2 | -1 | 0 | 1 | 2 |

| -7 | -6 | -5 | -4 | -3 | -2 | -1 | 0 | 1 | 2 |

| -7 | -6 | -5 | -4 | -3 | -2 | -1 | 0 | 1 | 2 |

Solve these equations without graphing them.

5. $4 + u = 2$ $u = \underline{\quad}$

6. $9c - 12 = 15c - 12$ $c = \underline{\quad}$

7. $2i + 8 = 18$ $i = \underline{\quad}$

8. $6b - 8 = 4 - 6b$ $b = \underline{\quad}$

$$\overline{\quad}_{1} \ \overline{\quad}_{0} \ \overline{\quad}_{5} \ \overline{\quad}_{-5} \ \overline{\quad}_{-7}$$

$$\overline{\quad}_{2} \ \overline{\quad}_{-1} \ \overline{\quad}_{-2}$$

TRENCHES-How deep are they?

BACKGROUND INFORMATION: It is hard to imagine that there is a trench 35,840 feet deep, and its beginning point is the ocean basin floor. This well-known trench is called the Mariana Trench and is located in the Pacific Ocean. Did you know there are several other trenches almost as deep as this one? In fact, there are some 22 deep-sea trenches in the Pacific Ocean, 3 in the Atlantic, and 1 in the Indian Ocean.

DIRECTIONS: Using the data given below, construct a bar graph comparing the depth of some of the world's deepest trenches. The numbers used in the chart have been rounded to the nearest hundred. Part of the graph has been constructed for you.

Some of the Oceans' Deepest Trenches

Name of trench	Depth	Name of trench	Depth
Mariana(Pacific)	35,800 ft.	Tonga(Pacific)	35,400 ft.
Phillipine(Pacific)	33,000 ft.	Kermadic(Pacific)	33,000 ft.
Puerto Rico Trench(Atlantic)	28,200 ft.	Romanche Gap(Atlantic)	25,400 ft.
Java (Indian)	23,400 ft.		

Title of Graph:_____

36,000 ft

20,000 ft

Mariana

NAME_____

How fast can fish swim and how long can they live?

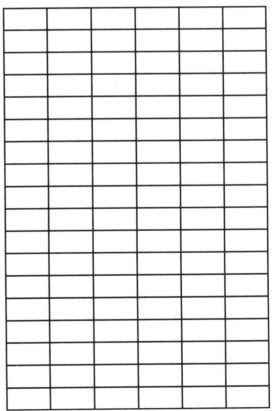

BACKGROUND INFORMATION: It's hard to imagine a fish moving along at 65 mph, but that's exactly what a tuna can do when swimming away from danger. <u>And</u>, can you imagine a fish living to be over 100 years old. There are records to show that a Koi(distant relative of the goldfish) has done just that. Use the data given below and construct two <u>line</u> graphs, one which will show average speeds of fish and the other graph will show their life spans.

Life Span of Several Long-Living Fish

NAME OF FISH	AVERAGE LIFE SPAN
Common Eel	88 years
Sturgeon	82 years
Koi	75 years
Pike	55 years
Carp	50 years
Goldfish	41 years
Tope(shark)	32 years

Speeds of Several Speedy Fish

NAME OF FISH	AVERAGE SPEED
Swordfish	68 mph
Yellowfish tuna	46 mph
Flying Fish	45 mph
Tuna	43 mph
Trout	15 mph
Salmon	11 mph

Title:

Title:

Graphing positive and negative coordinates

What marsupial is called the "old man" in Australia?

BACKGROUND INFORMATION: I can reach a weight of 200 pounds and a length of ten feet from my nose to the tip of my tail. I can leap along the ground at 30 miles an hour. My young is called a joey and it's only 1 inch long when born. It finds shelter in my pouch where my muscles pump milk down its throat. At four months old my joey can climb out of the pouch and nibble grass; however, if danger threatens , I will move at full speed, gather it up and tuck it into my pouch.

What am I? _____

DIRECTIONS: This graph has positive and negative coordinates. It is made up of 5 lines. The symbol [denotes the beginning of a line and the symbol] the end of a line. Graph the coordinates in the order given below.

[(8,1), (10,1), (11,2), (12,5), (12,2), (13,5), (13,2), (15,1), (16,0), (16,-1), (15,0), (15,-1), (14,-1), (12,0), (9,-2), (7,-3),]   [(5,1), (6,2), (7,2), (8,1), (8,-1), (7,-3), (7,-4), (5,-3), (4,-5), (1,-5), (2,-4), (3,-4), (3,-3) (4,-1), (6,-2), (5,0)] [(0,-2), (2,-3), (3,-3] (-1,3), (-2,3), (1,1), (1,0), (0,-2), (-2,-7), (-1,-9), (0,-10), (2,-11), (3,-12), (1,-12), (-4,-7), (-3,-3), (-7,-1), (-4,-4), (-5,-7), (0,-12), (1,-12)]   [(6,2), (4,3), (0,6), (-2,6) (-4,5), (-7,3), (-10,1), (-14,-3), (-17,-4), (-20,-4), (-17,-5), (-12,-4), (-8,-2), (-7,-1)].

Now, draw an eye like this ⊙ around (13,1).

Graphing coordinates

NAME_____

CREATING A GRAPH

DIRECTIONS: Think of many, varied and unusual objects, designs, or even characters that could be used as the subject of your graph. Once you have reached your decision, here are some guidelines.

1. Your graph should contain a minimium of 30 ordered pairs(coordinates).
2. You will need to write clear directions so that a classmate could follow them and recreate your graph.
3. After you have finished designing and writing out your coordinates with directions, you will need to make sure your graph works by doing it again on another sheet of graph paper.

COORDINATES WITH DIRECTIONS

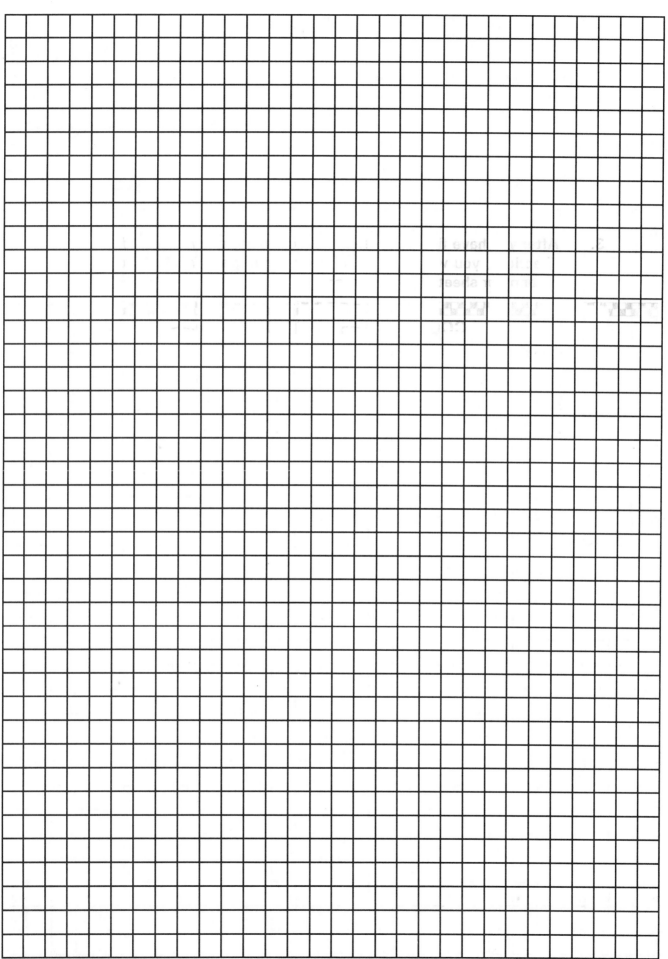

NAME_____

AREA: USE YOUR IMAGINATION

DIRECTIONS: Use your imagination and create shapes on the
graph paper that will show you understand the concept of area.
(1) Create 3 different shapes that have an area of 8 square units.

(2) Create 3 different shapes that have an area of 12 square units.

(3) Create 2 different shapes that have an area of 15 square units.

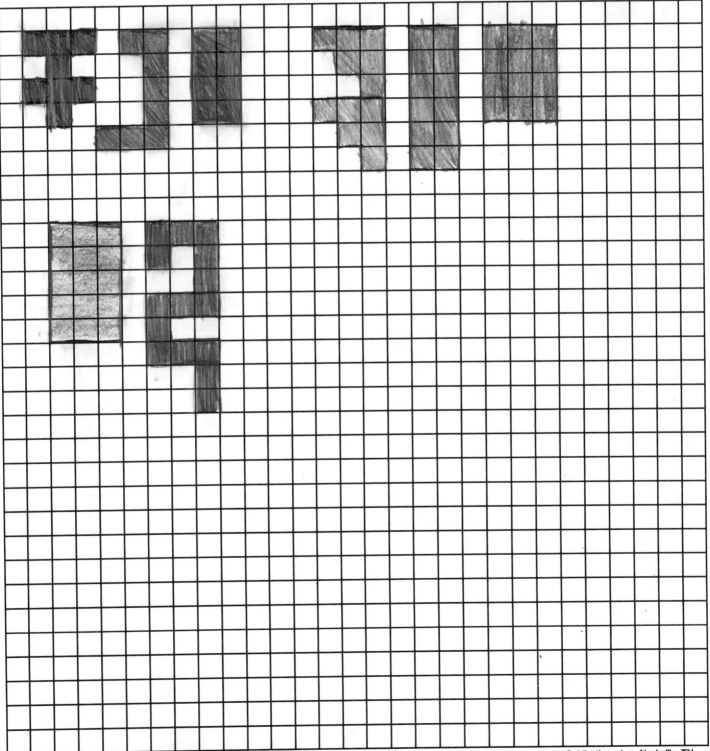

NAME_____

Graphing Equations

DIRECTIONS: Complete each table and then graph each solution.

1.

x	-2x + 4	y
1		
2		
3		
4		

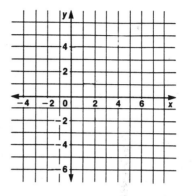

2.

x	y = x + 1	y
-1		
0		
3		
5		

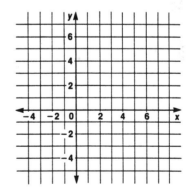

3.

x	$\frac{2}{3}x + 2$	y
-3		
0		
3		
6		

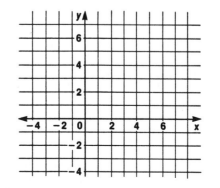

4.

x	$\frac{1}{2}x - 1$	y
0		
1		
2		
3		

NAME_____

SLOPES

DIRECTIONS: Find the slope of each line.

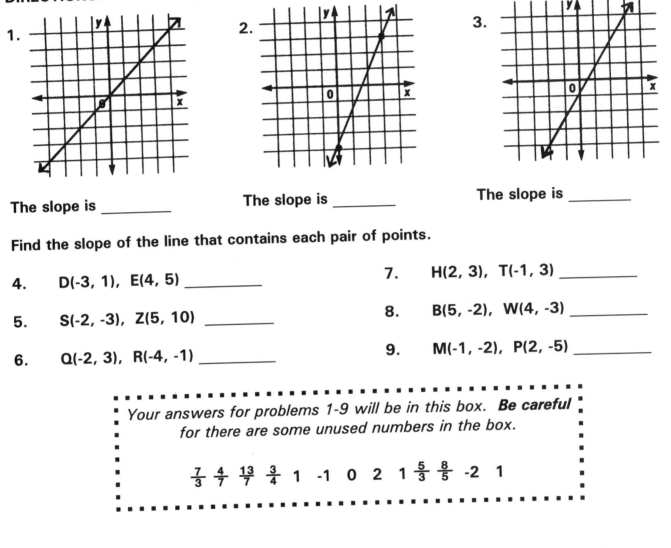

1.

The slope is _____

2.

The slope is _____

3.

The slope is _____

Find the slope of the line that contains each pair of points.

4.   D(-3, 1), E(4, 5) _____

5.   S(-2, -3), Z(5, 10) _____

6.   Q(-2, 3), R(-4, -1) _____

7.   H(2, 3), T(-1, 3) _____

8.   B(5, -2), W(4, -3) _____

9.   M(-1, -2), P(2, -5) _____

Your answers for problems 1-9 will be in this box. **Be careful** for there are some unused numbers in the box.

$$\frac{7}{3} \quad \frac{4}{7} \quad \frac{13}{7} \quad \frac{3}{4} \quad 1 \quad -1 \quad 0 \quad 2 \quad 1\frac{5}{3} \quad \frac{8}{5} \quad -2 \quad 1$$

Graph the line containing each pair of points, and then state the slope of the line.

10.   (2, 1), (0, -1)

11.   (2, -3), (-3, 2)

12.   (2, -1), (2, 3)

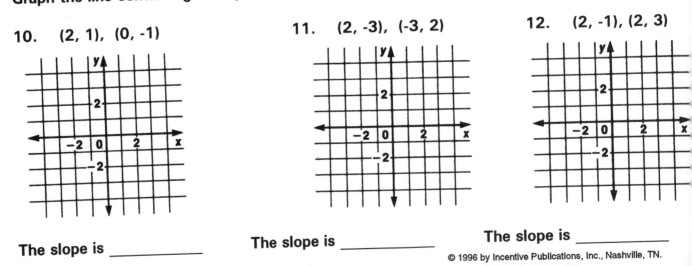

The slope is _____

The slope is _____

The slope is _____

INTERCEPTS

DIRECTIONS: Find the x-intercept and y-intercept for the graph of each equation.

1. $y = x - 4$
y int. = ____   x int. = ____

2. $y = 3x - 4$
y int. = ____   x int. = ____

3. $y = 12 - 6x$
y int. = ____   x int. = ____

4. $y = 2 - 3x$
y int. = ____   x int. = ____

5. $y = 8 - 2x$
y int. = ____   x int. = ____

6. $y = -x - 3$
y int. = ____   x int. = ____

> *Possible answers for problems 1-6*
>
> y int. = -4, x int. = $\frac{4}{3}$ y int. = 2, x int. = $\frac{2}{3}$ y int. = -8, x int. = 2
>
> y int. = 12, x int. = 2   y int. = -3, x int. = $\frac{1}{3}$ y int. = -3, x int. = -3
>
> y int. = 8, x int. = 4   y int. = -4, x int. = 4

Use the x-intercept and the y-intercept to graph each equation.

7. $y = 2x + 3$

8. $y = 0.5x + 2$

9. $y = x + 3$

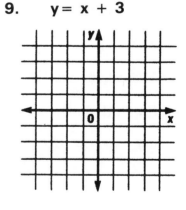

10. $y = 2x + 4$

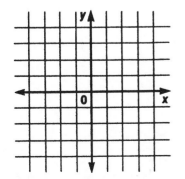

11. $y = x - 1$

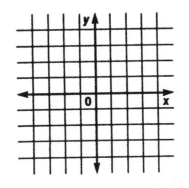

12. $y = \frac{1}{2}x - 2$

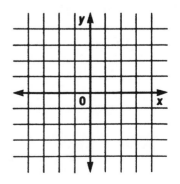

NAME_____

Why do teachers take aspirin?

DIRECTIONS: Express each ratio as a unit rate. Then, find your answer in the decoder. Each time your answer occurs, write the letter of the problem above it.

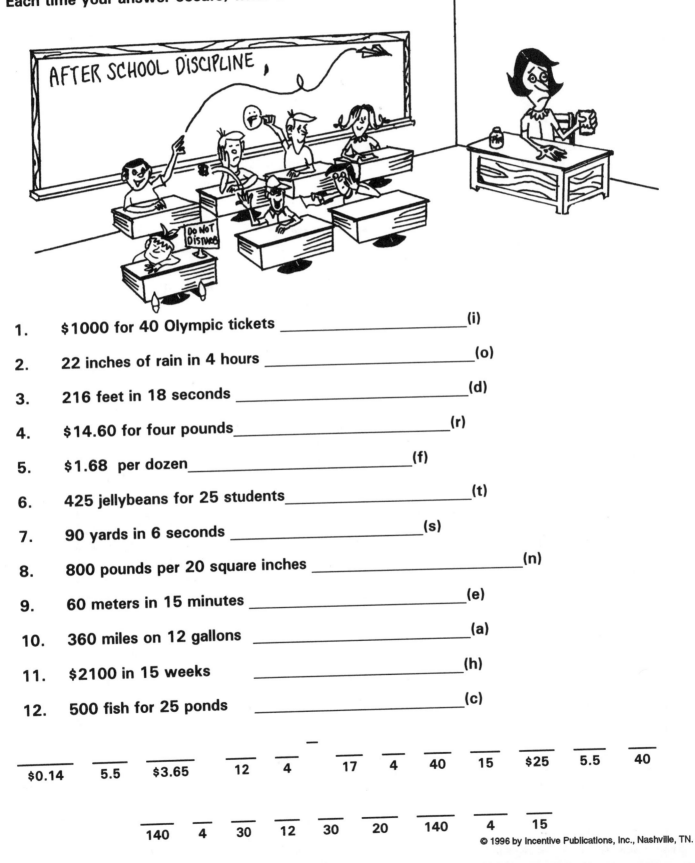

1. $1000 for 40 Olympic tickets _____ (i)

2. 22 inches of rain in 4 hours _____ (o)

3. 216 feet in 18 seconds _____ (d)

4. $14.60 for four pounds_____ (r)

5. $1.68 per dozen_____ (f)

6. 425 jellybeans for 25 students_____ (t)

7. 90 yards in 6 seconds _____ (s)

8. 800 pounds per 20 square inches _____ (n)

9. 60 meters in 15 minutes _____ (e)

10. 360 miles on 12 gallons _____ (a)

11. $2100 in 15 weeks _____ (h)

12. 500 fish for 25 ponds _____ (c)

___
—
___ ___ ___ ___ ___ ___ ___ ___ ___ ___ ___
$0.14 5.5 $3.65 12 4 17 4 40 15 $25 5.5 40

___ ___ ___ ___ ___ ___ ___ ___ ___
140 4 30 12 30 20 140 4 15

NAME _____

Cross Products: An Easy Way to Determine Proportions

Examine these proportions:

$$\frac{2}{3} = \frac{8}{12}$$

$2 \times 12 = 8 \times 3$

$24 = 24$

(This is a proportion)

$$\frac{3}{5} = \frac{7}{10}$$

$3 \times 10 \neq 7 \times 5$

$30 \neq 35$

(This is not a proportion)

Use cross products - it's the easy way!

DIRECTIONS: Use cross products to see if each of the following equations are proportions. Put a check (✓) by those equations that are proportions.

1. $\dfrac{3}{4} = \dfrac{15}{20}$

2. $\dfrac{3}{7} = \dfrac{6}{13}$

3. $\dfrac{8}{9} = \dfrac{32}{36}$

4. $\dfrac{35}{50} = \dfrac{7}{10}$

5. $\dfrac{3}{7} = \dfrac{21}{42}$

6. $\dfrac{8}{7} = \dfrac{21}{24}$

7. $\dfrac{6}{7} = \dfrac{18}{22}$

8. $\dfrac{3}{9} = \dfrac{24}{72}$

9. $\dfrac{11}{12} = \dfrac{44}{48}$

10. $\dfrac{25}{75} = \dfrac{1}{4}$

11. $\dfrac{12}{48} = \dfrac{1}{4}$

12. $\dfrac{7}{9} = \dfrac{21}{27}$

13. $\dfrac{14}{16} = \dfrac{42}{48}$

14. $\dfrac{6}{7} = \dfrac{18}{22}$

Helpful hint: You should have 8 checks!

Using proportions

NAME _____

What does Thomas Jefferson call a note excusing you from school?

DIRECTIONS: Write a proportion that could be used to solve for each variable. Then solve and find your answer in the decoder. Each time it occurs write the letter of the problem above it.

1. 3 tires at $240
   p tires at $400

   $p =$ ____

2. 1 gallon of orange juice weighs 7½ lbs
   20 gallons of juice weighs r pounds

   $r =$ ____

3. 4 kg of hamburger will serve 20 people
   e kg of hamburger will serve 100 people

   $e =$ ____

4. 135 miles on 3 gallons of gas
   o miles on 9 gallons of gas

   $o =$ ____

5. 4 kittens at $22.00
   6 kitten at i dollars

   $i =$ ____

6. 6 cups of flour for 80 cookies
   n cups of flour for 100 cookies

   $n =$ ____

7. 10 acre field produces 250 bushels of corn
   25 acre field produces t bushels of corn

   $t =$ ____

8. 4 packages of cheese at $6.80
   7 packages of cheese for a dollars

   $a =$ ____

9. 200 miles in 2.5 days
   l miles in 12 days

   $l =$ ____

10. 2 motorbikes at $1890
    7 motorbikes at c

    $c =$ ____

11. 30 cm by 50 cm reduced
    to 15 cm by d cm

    $d =$ ____

12. 3 magazines for $10.50
    12 magazines for f dollars

    $f =$ ____

—————— —————— —————— —————— —————— —————— —————— ——————
11.90   25   20 $6,615   960 $11.90   150 $11.90

—————— —————— —————— —————— —————— —————— —————— ——————
405      $42 $33   7.5   25   5   20   7.5

—————— —————— —————— —————— —————— ——————
625      $33   405   7.5

—————— —————— —————— ——————
20   25   20 $6,615   20   20

Using the percent proportion

Why do some say that whales talk too much?

DIRECTIONS: Use a proportion to solve each problem. Locate your answer in the decoder, and each time your answer occurs in the decoder write the letter of the problem above it.

1. What number is 75% of 800? _____ (p)

2. Find 60% of 90. _____ (r)

3. What number is 50% of 84? _____ (e)

4. Find 24% of 10.5. _____ (g)

5. 36 is what percent of 24? _____ (h)

6. Find 86.5% of 100. _____ (w)

7. 60 is 75% of what number? _____ (a)

8. 8% of 2000 is _____ (y)

9. 39 is 40% of what number? _____ (s)

10. What is 37.5% of 300? _____ (n)

11. Of the 600 peaches in Morgan's orchard, 60% will be sold to a local fruit stand. How many will be sold? _____ (o)

12. Eighty percent of the tickets for the baseball game on July 4th have been sold. There are 20,000 tickets. How many have been sold? _____ (i)

13. Nathan's income is $225.00 per week. He is saving 90% for a new car. How much is he saving per week? _____ (u)

14. In order to make an A on his pre-algebra test, Reid needs to get 92% of the problems correct. If there are 50 problems on the test, how many does he need to get correct? _____ (l)

15. In a used car lot in Michigan, 40% of the vehicles had areas containing rust. If there were 185 cars in the lot, how many had rust? _____ (t)

16. 7% of 3000 is what number? _____ (f)

74	150%	42	160	80	54	42	80	46	86.5	80	160	97.5

97.5	600	360	202.50	74	16,000	112.5	2.52	360	210	210

NAME_____

Why is a bell the most obedient thing in the world?

DIRECTIONS: Use your estimating skills to determine the best estimate for the problems below. Find your estimate in the decoder. Each time it occurs in the decoder write the letter of the problem above it.

1. 9% of 45 = _____ (v)

2. $9\frac{7}{8}$% of 50 = _____ (i)

3. $\frac{6}{7}$% of 75 = _____ (a)

4. $4\frac{2}{3}$% of $58 = _____ (u)

5. 195% of 800 = _____ (e)

6. 1.2% of 98 = _____ (k)

7. 0.9% of 1,470 = _____ (d)

8. 66% of 155 = _____ (r)

Estimate to find the percent:

9. 9 out of 198 = _____ (p)

10. 15 out of 21 = _____ (o)

11. 9 out of 91 = _____ (s)

12. 18 out of 80 = _____ (n)

13. 22 out of 100 = _____ (l)

14. 15 out of 24 = _____ (t)

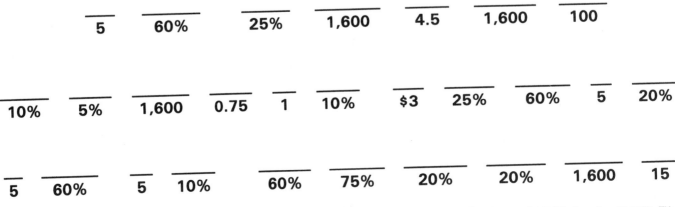

__5__	__60%__	__25%__	__1,600__	__4.5__	__1,600__	__100__

__10%__	__5%__	__1,600__	__0.75__	__1__	__10%__	__$3__	__25%__	__60%__	__5__	__20%__

__5__	__60%__	__5__	__10%__	__60%__	__75%__	__20%__	__20%__	__1,600__	__15__

What did one chick say to the other chick after their mother laid an orange instead of an egg?

DIRECTIONS: Using an equation solve each of these percent problems. Find your answer in the decoder. Each time your answer occurs in the decoder, write the letter of the problem above it.

NAME _____

1. 90.5 is 25% of what number? _____ (t)

2. 42 is 60% of what number? _____ (n)

3. 15 is what percent of 75? _____ (h)

4. 125% of what number is 15? _____ (k)

5. Find 200% of 136. _____ (o)

6. What number is 30% of 120? _____ (a)

7. 2 is what percent of 125? _____ (l)

8. 8 is 10% of what number? _____ (e)

9. Gina's Dad earned a 3% commission on all the motorcycles he sold. In November, he earned $375 in commissions. What were his total sales? _____ (r)

10. Sarah purchased a set of art supplies for $20.90 and a pair of jeans for $18.95. The sales tax rate in the state is 7%. How much change did Sarah receive from $50? _____ (d)

11. Jon purchased a skateboard for $69. If the sales tax is $5.52, what is the sales tax rate? _____ (g)

12. You earned a 15% commission on the magazines you sold. Your first month sales were $200. How much in commission did you earn? _____ (m)

1.6%	272	272	12	36	362	362	$12,500	80	20%	362	272	$12,500	36	70	80

$30	36	36	$12,500	$30	36	1.6%	36	$7.36	80	8%

© 1996 by Incentive Publications, Inc., Nashville, TN.

NAME_____

Estimating Percents

DIRECTIONS: Complete the table below by using your estimating skills. The chart at the right can be helpful in providing you with the percent equivalents for commonly used fractions. An example has been done for you.

Actual no.	*Rounded no.*	*Fractional equivalent*	*Estimate will be a little:*
13%	$12\frac{1}{2}$%	$\frac{1}{8}$	less

Actual number	Rounded number	Fractional equivalent	Is your estimate a little less or a little more?
1. 34%			
2. 89%			
3. 22%			
4. 99%			
5. 61%			
6. 77%			
7. 88%			
8. 24%			
9. 37%			
10. 13%			
11. 69%			
12. 48%			

$\frac{1}{2}$ = 50%

$\frac{1}{3}$ = $33\frac{1}{3}$ %

$\frac{2}{3}$ = $66\frac{2}{3}$ %

$\frac{1}{4}$ = 25%

$\frac{3}{4}$ = 75%

$\frac{1}{5}$ = 20%

$\frac{2}{5}$ = 40%

$\frac{3}{5}$ = 60%

$\frac{4}{5}$ = 80%

$\frac{1}{8}$ = $12\frac{1}{2}$ %

$\frac{3}{8}$ = $37\frac{1}{2}$ %

$\frac{5}{8}$ = $62\frac{1}{2}$ %

$\frac{7}{8}$ = $87\frac{1}{2}$ %

$\frac{1}{10}$ = 10%

$\frac{3}{10}$ = 30%

$\frac{7}{10}$ = 70%

$\frac{9}{10}$ = 90%

What makes a piano laugh?

DIRECTIONS: Solve each problem. Find your answer in the decoder. Each time your answer occurs in the decoder, write the letter of the problem above it.

Express each fraction as a percent.

1. $\frac{17}{50}$ = h   (h = _____)

2. $\frac{11}{12}$ = n   (n = _____)

3. $\frac{6}{5}$ = l   (l = _____)

4. $\frac{5}{2}$ = m   (m = _____)

Express each decimal as a percent.

5. 0.204 = r   (r = _____)

6. 0.07 = g   (g = _____)

7. 0.006 = c   (c = _____)

8. 1.043 = k   (k = _____)

Express each percent as a fraction in simplest form.

9. 48% = o   (o = _____)

10. 2.5% = v   (v = _____)

11. 87.5% = e   (e = _____)

Express each percent as a decimal

12. 12% = t   (t = _____)

13. 33.3% = s   (s = _____)

14. 13.5 % = i   (i = _____)

Decoder row 1 (top right):
$\overline{}$ 7% $\overline{}$ $91\frac{2}{3}\%$ $\overline{}$ 0.135 $\overline{}$ 120% $\overline{}$ 104.3% $\overline{}$ 0.6% $\overline{}$ 0.135 $\overline{}$ 0.12

Decoder row 2:
$\overline{}$ $0.33\frac{1}{3}$ $\overline{}$ $\frac{7}{8}$ $\overline{}$ 0.135 $\overline{}$ 20.4% $\overline{}$ $\frac{12}{25}$ $\overline{}$ $\frac{1}{40}$

Decoder row 3 (bottom left area):
$\overline{}$ $\frac{7}{8}$ $\overline{}$ $91\frac{2}{3}\%$ $\overline{}$ $\frac{7}{8}$ $\overline{}$ $\frac{12}{25}$ $\overline{}$ 250% $\overline{}$ 34%

Decoder row 4 (bottom):
$\overline{}$ $0.33\frac{1}{3}$ $\overline{}$ $\frac{12}{25}$ $\overline{}$ 0.12

64

NAME _____

What are the fastest ways of sending news?

DIRECTIONS: Solve each problem. Find your answer in the decoder. Each time your answer occurs in the decoder write the letter of the problem above it.

Find the discount or interest to the nearest cent.

1. $1575 computer, 30% off   Discount is _____ (d)

2. $195 skateboard, 40% off   Discount is _____ (n)

3. $495 for a compact disc player, 20% off   Discount is _____ (h)

4. $1,050 for a CD Rom, 25% off   Discount is _____ (a)

5. $700 at 8% for 1 year   Interest is _____ (e)

6. $40,000 at 12% for 15 years   Interest is _____ (l)

7. $30,000 at 5% for 10 years   Interest is _____ (v)

8. $1,270 at 18% for 2 years   Interest is _____ (p)

Find the discount rate. Round to the nearest whole percent.

9. $15 compact disc on sale for $9   Discount rate is _____ (o)

10. $30 book bag on sale for $22   Discount rate is _____ (s)

11. $36 sweater on sale for $25   Discount rate is _____ (i)

12. $9 cassette tape on sale for $5.95   Discount rate is _____ (g)

13. $59.95 tennis shoes on sale for $39.95   Discount rate is _____ (t)

___	___	___	___	___	___	___	___	___
33%	56	72,000	56	457.20	99	40%	78	56

___	___	___	___	___	___	___	___	___	___
33%	56	72,000	56	15,000	31%	27%	31%	40%	78

___	___	___
262.50	78	472.50

___	___	___	___	___
33%	56	72,000	72,000	262.50

___	___	___	___	___	___
34%	40%	27%	27%	31%	457.20

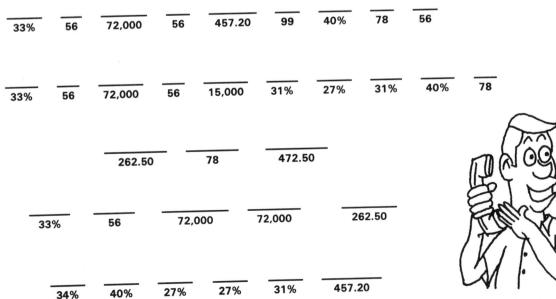

Percent of change

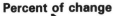

Why does an empty wallet always stay empty?

DIRECTIONS: Find the percent of change in the problems below. Round to the nearest whole percent.

7. old: $57.30
    new: $37.60
    percent of change = _____(e)

8. old: $150
    new: $135
    percent of change = _____(s)

1. old: $325
    new: $375
    percent of change = _____(y)

9. old: $3.00
    new: $3.60
    percent of change = _____(t)

2. old: $65.00
    new: $68.25
    percent of change = _____(r)

10. old: $16
    new: $28
    percent of change = _____(c)

3. old: $75
    new: $85
    percent of change = _____(v)

11. $38 sweater increased to $48
    percent of increase = _____(h)

12. old: $2,200
    new: $1,600
    percent of change = _____(n)

4. Greg weighed 140 pounds. On his diet he lost 15 pounds. What was the percent of decrease in Greg's weight? _____(g)

5. You can warm up your spaghetti on a gas range in 10 minutes. You can warm up that same spaghetti in the microwave in 2 minutes. Find the percent of decrease in cooking time. _____(a)

6. A $12 cassette disc is increased to $18.00. What is the percent of increase?_____(i)

20%	26%	34%	5%	34%	50%	10%	27%	34%	13%	34%	5%

80%	27%	15%	75%	26%	80%	27%	11%	34%	50%	27%	50%	20%

NAME_____

The Collection of Data

DIRECTIONS: Use the data given below and complete the charts. The first one has been done for you.

INFO: The scores for a student's semester science grades are: 55, 75, 85, 65, 70, 95, 55, 83, 85, 100, 97, 85.

1. Complete the frequency portion of the chart to the right.

2. What is the highest score? _____

3. What is the lowest score? _____

4. What is the frequency of the score that occurred most often? _____

5. How many scores are 70 or higher? _____

6. If 70 is the lowest passing score, how many scores are not passing? _____

7. What is this student's average for the semester? _____

Score	Tally	Frequency
95-100	III	3
90-94		
85-89	III	
80-84	I	
75-79	I	
70-74	I	
Below 70	III	

Use the frequency table to the right to complete this section.

8. Complete the frequency portion of this table.

9. How many people responded to this survey? _____

10. What is the ratio of those students who watch 2-3 hours of television per day to those who watch 1-2 hours per day? _____

11. What percent of students watch television 3-4 hours per day?

_____

Hours per day viewing television in the summer	Tally	Frequency
0 hours	⊞⊞ I	
0 - ½ hours	⊞⊞ IIII	
1-2 hours	⊞⊞ ⊞⊞ III	
2-3 hours	⊞⊞ ⊞⊞ I	
3-4 hours	⊞⊞ I	
5-6 hours	III	
6 or more hours	II	

EXTENSION: *Choose an activity for which you could collect data. Organize your data by making a chart similar to those used on this page.*

NAME_____

Why do weeping willows weep?

DIRECTIONS: Solve each of the problems. Find your answer in the decoder and each time it occurs write the letter of the problem above it.

Find the median(middle number)

1. 3.6, 3.9, 4.2, 2.5, 6.7 _____(f)

2. 10.34, 10.56, 10.21, 10.84, 10.57 _____ (h)

3. 1.0321, 1.6784, 1.0341, 1.1421, 1.0093 _____(y)

Find the mean(average)

7. 76, 54, 97, 83, 61 _____(l)

8. 10.3, 10.9, 10.6, 10.1, 10.5 _____(t)

9. 146, 148, 149, 162, 184, 189_____(r)

Find the mode(occurs most often)

4. 67, 67, 68, 69, 30, 45, 81 _____(s)

5. 1.43, 1.41, 1.41, 1.4, 1.41, 1.43, _____ (o)

6. 5.6, 5.7, 5.8, 5.7, 5.3 _____ (e)

Use the table to answer these questions

10. What is the median of Lisse's scores? _____(a)

11. What is the mode of her scores? _____(n)

12. What is the mean? _____(i)

13. If Lisse needs to average 90 for an "A", how many points above 90 is her average?_____(p)

Lisse's Math Test Scores	
97	96
98	97
84	89
85	92
88	

10.48	10.56	5.7	1.0341

3.9	5.7	5.7	74.2	3.9	1.41	163

10.48	10.56	5.7	1.8	91.8	97	5.7

10.48	163	5.7	5.7	67

10.48	10.56	92	10.48

1.8	91.8	97	5.7

NAME _____

Finding mean, mode, and median

YOU ARE THE TEACHER!!

DIRECTIONS: You are the teacher, and it's time to average all those grades. The class is Pre-algebra I. Get your calculator, and you're ready to go. You will first add the grades for each student, then average them, and finally use the grading scale to assign a grade for that grading period. Round the average(mean) to the nearest whole number. The first one has been done for you.

	M	T	W	TH	F	M	T	W	TH	F	M	T	W	TH	F	Total Points	Average	Final Grade	Grading Scale
Tisha	98	80	84		96		100		95	94	92		100	95	95	1,029	94	A	92-100 A
Cory	65	74	81		70		75		92	81	99		60	82	90				
Mark	60	55	72		74		50		65	74	75		80	92	100				83-91 B
Nathan	45	60	0		60		55		72	84	70		85	87	92				
Forrest	100	94	95		100		98		100	85	102		97	101	99				
Angela	85	90	65		100		75		85	90	70		100	96	95				74-82 C
Maria	90	0	60		85		90		79	85	0		100	95	85				
Earl	70	75	0		65		80		75	85	100		100	100	92				
Kyung	100	101	101		95		100		98	102	97		101	103	99				70-73 D
Jeff	85	100	75		85		0		95	75	85		100	85	91				
Dementra	90	85	100		85		95		100	85	92		95	100	89				
Jenny	60	95	0		95		80		80	80	95		85	90	85				
Sinbad	95	95	90		92		85		100	95	92		100	94	94				Below 70 F

1. What is the median of the class's score? _____

2. What is the mode? _____ What is the mean? _____

3. Interpret Jeff's scores: median _____, mode _____, mean _____

4. Progress reports are sent home after two weeks to students earning 70% or below. List those students who will receive a progress report.

5. How do you suppose Kyung had grades greater than 100?

6. A zero indicates that assignments were not turned in. How many students had zeros in their averages? _____ Do you think zeros significantly affect an average? _____ Examine Nathan's scores. If the zero were changed to a 70, how would that have affected his overall average?

7. How would Maria's grade have changed if she had made 70's in place of her two zeros?

NAME_____

TREE DIAGRAMS

DIRECTIONS: Make a tree diagram for each exercise. Find the number of possible outcomes. An example has been done for you.

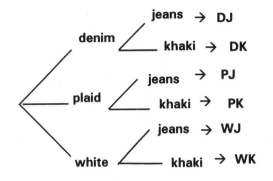

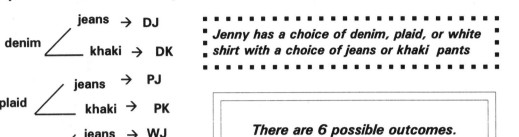

Jenny has a choice of denim, plaid, or white shirt with a choice of jeans or khaki pants

There are 6 possible outcomes.

1. At the yogurt shop you have a choice of strawberry, banana, or vanilla yogurt with choice of one topping. Your choice of toppings include strawberries, walnuts, or M & M's. Possible outcomes are _____.

2. Soccer uniforms come in three sizes, small, medium, large. The basic colors are gold, black, red, and orange. Possible outcomes are _____.

3. School folders come in 3 colors, black, red, and purple. They come in 2 styles, one with pockets and no brads, and one with pockets and brads. Possible outcomes are _____.

4. As part of a unit on the Revolutionary War, students in Mrs. Spiller's class were given a choice of three books to read, *My Brother Sam is Dead*, *Johnny Tremain* or *Toliver's Secret*. They were also asked to choose an accompanying project, a diorama, dress up as a character, or make a model. Possible outcomes are _____.

NAME_____

How does a quiet Hawaiian laugh?

DIRECTIONS: Use the *Fundamental Counting Principle* to determine the possible outcomes. Find your possible outcomes answer in the decoder and write the letter of the problem above it.

> ### Example
> Nicole gets to choose her own phone for her birthday. Her choices are a wall, or desk phone, rotary, or touch tone phone, and colors of black, beige, white or red. How many combinations are possible?   **2 x 2 x 4 = 16**

1. Five dice are rolled. How many possible outcomes? _____(h)

2. If Michelle has 4 skirts, 3 blouses, and 2 sweaters, how many outfits are possible?   _____(t)

3. There are 5 movies playing at the local theater. Each is showing at four different times. How many choices are possible? _____(w)

4. There are 6 pitchers and 3 catchers on a baseball team of 25 players. How many possible pitcher-catcher combinations? _____(i)

5. At Philly Connection there is a choice of 12 sandwiches, 6 drinks, and 4 different kinds of chips. How many combinations are available if you order one sandwich, one drink, and one bag of chips? _____(o)

6. If your teacher gives you an eight question true-false test, how many sets of answers are possible? _____(a)

7. Jenny's family is planning a trip to Orlando, Florida, for 3 days. While there they can choose to go to the beach, Sea World, Disneyworld, MGM Studios, or deep sea fishing. How many combinations are possible if they choose to do only one activity for each of the three days? _____(l)

___	___	___	___	___	___	___	___	___	___
20	18	24	7,776	256	15	288	20	7,776	256

NAME_____

WHAT'S THE PROBABILITY?

BACKGROUND INFORMATION: Each day we are affected by probability. What's the probability it will rain? What's the probability I will have a test in math? Is there a chance I will ever win the lottery? We know that some events are almost 100% probable. Others may happen and are about 50% probable. *And,* there are other events that have a very low probability of ever occurring.

Think of many varied and unusual events that would fit in each of the 3 categories below.

??????????   HIGH PROBABILITY (These events will most likely occur)   **?????????**

1.	6.
2.	7.
3.	8.
4.	9.
5.	10.

??????????   AVERAGE PROBABILITY(These events might occur and they might not—about a 50% probability)   **?????????**

1.	6.
2.	7.
3.	8.
4.	9.
5.	10.

???????????   LOW PROBABILITY(These events will probably not occur)   **?????????**

1.	6.
2.	7.
3.	8.
4.	9.
5.	10.

NAME_____

What's the probability?

Directions: We can use multicolored, candy-coated chocolates to enhance our understanding of probability. First, predict the probability of getting each of the following colors if you randomly choose one piece from a small package or cup without looking at what you are choosing. Put your prediction in fractional form.

Red_____   Orange_____   Yellow_____

Green_____   Dark Brown_____   Light Brown_____

Now empty your candies out on your desk and separate them by colors. Complete the chart below. How many pieces were in your bag? _____

Color	How many of each color? *(Use tally marks to show your totals.)*	Fractional total in simplest form	Compare your outcome with your prediction. *(Was your outcome right on target, fairly close, or not close at all?)*
Red			
Yellow			
Orange			
Green			
Dark Brown			
Light Brown			

Interpretation of Data: Class Discussion Questions
1.   Did everyone in your class have the same number of pieces in his/her package? Yes__No__ If not, what is a possible reason why the packages would be different?

_____
2.   Was one color predominant in your class? Yes__No__ If so, which color? _____ What are some reasons why this might have occurred?_____

_____
3.   Analyzing the total numbers from your class, did one color appear to be used less often? Yes__No__ If so, what could be a reason?_____
4.   Write one or two statements about what you've learned about probability from this activity?_____

_____

What do you call a bungee jumper who is a thief?

DIRECTIONS: Measure the degrees in each angle and tell what kind of angle each is: acute, obtuse, right, or straight. Find the measurement of your angle in the answer key, and each time it occurs write the letter of the problem above it. The first one has been done for you.

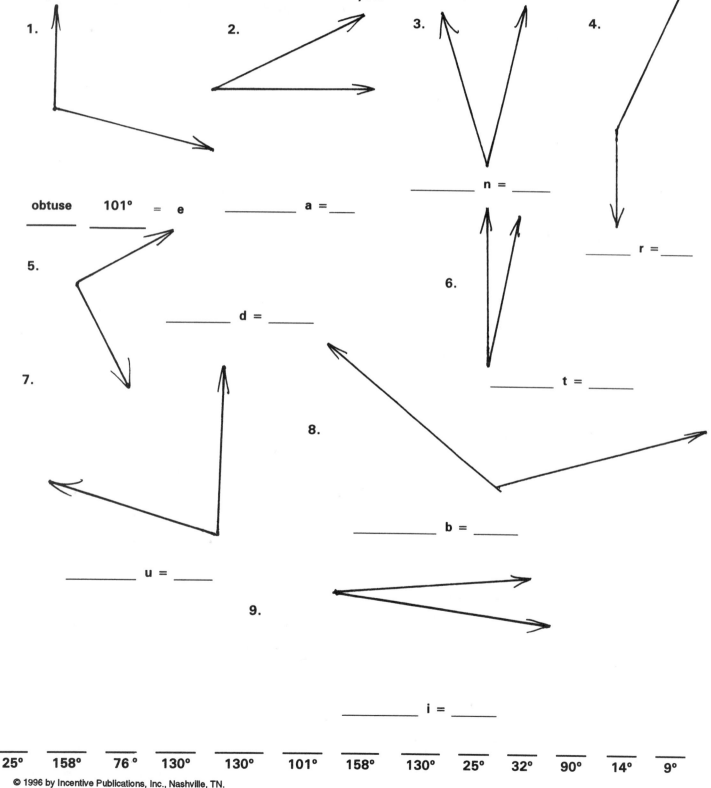

1.

2.

3.
_____ n = _____

4.

obtuse   101° = e   _____ a = ___

5.

_____ d = _____

6.

_____ r = ___

7.

_____ t = _____

8.

_____ b = _____

_____ u = ___

9.

_____ i = ___

_____ _____ _____ _____ _____ _____ _____ _____ _____ _____ _____ _____ _____
25°   158°   76°   130°   130°   101°   158°   130°   25°   32°   90°   14°   9°

TRIANGLES AND QUADRILATERALS

DIRECTIONS: All triangles have angles which, when added, total 180 degrees. All quadrilaterals have angles which, when totaled, measure 360 degrees. Measure each of the angles in these triangles and quadrilaterals and see how close to 180 or 360 degrees your measurements are. You may need to extend many of the lines of your angles to get an accurate measurement. Show your computations.

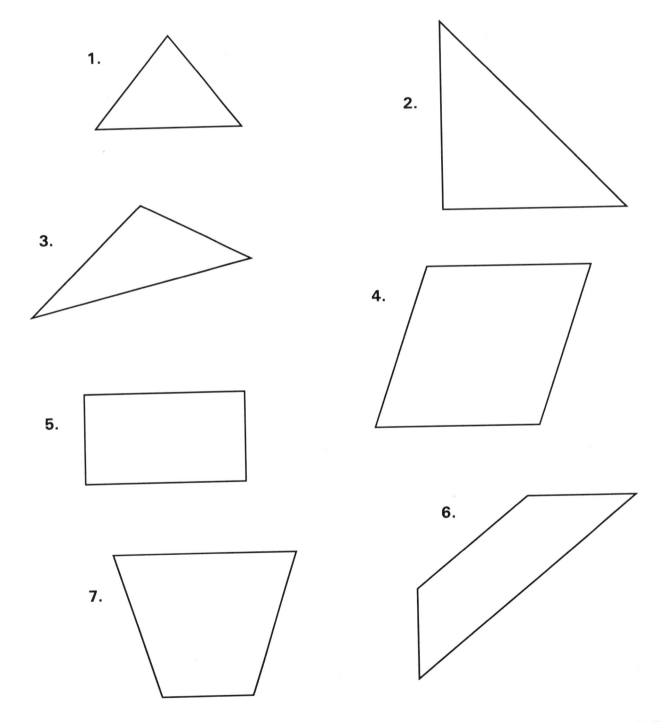

Using knowledge of polygons to create a machine

THE DREAM MACHINE

DIRECTIONS: Using your knowledge of polygons create your own "Dream Machine."
Use at least 10 different polygons in your design and be able to identify each one that is used.

List the different polygons used in creating your "Dream Machine."

1. _____   5. _____   9. _____
2. _____   6. _____   10. _____
3. _____   7. _____   11. _____
4. _____   8. _____   12. _____

Create an ad to market your "Dream Machine." Include in your ad the function of your machine.

NAME _____

Geometry in our environment

SHAPES SCAVENGER HUNT

DIRECTIONS: Take a tour of your school and search for the many, varied and unusual shapes you can find both inside and outside your school building. Record in the chart the things that you found under the name of each shape's name. Try to find at least 3 in each category.

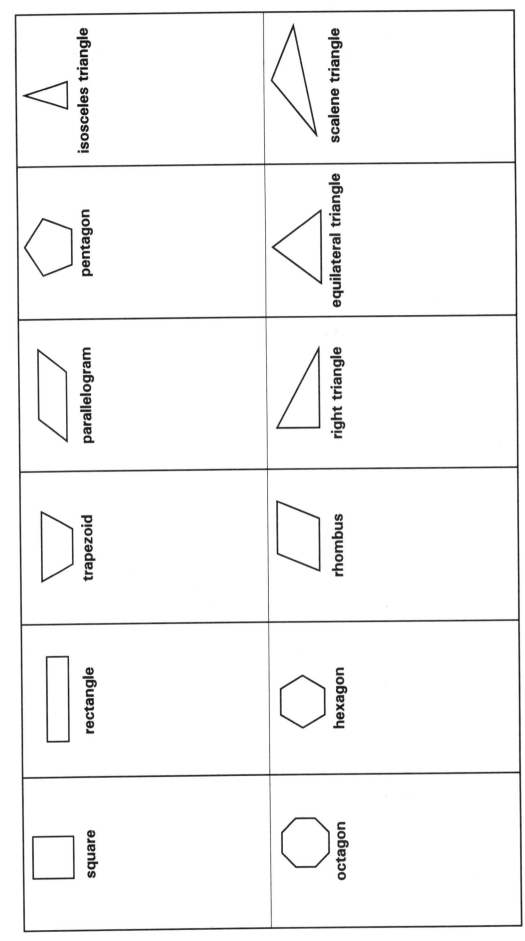

NAME_____

What's a cannibal's favorite game?

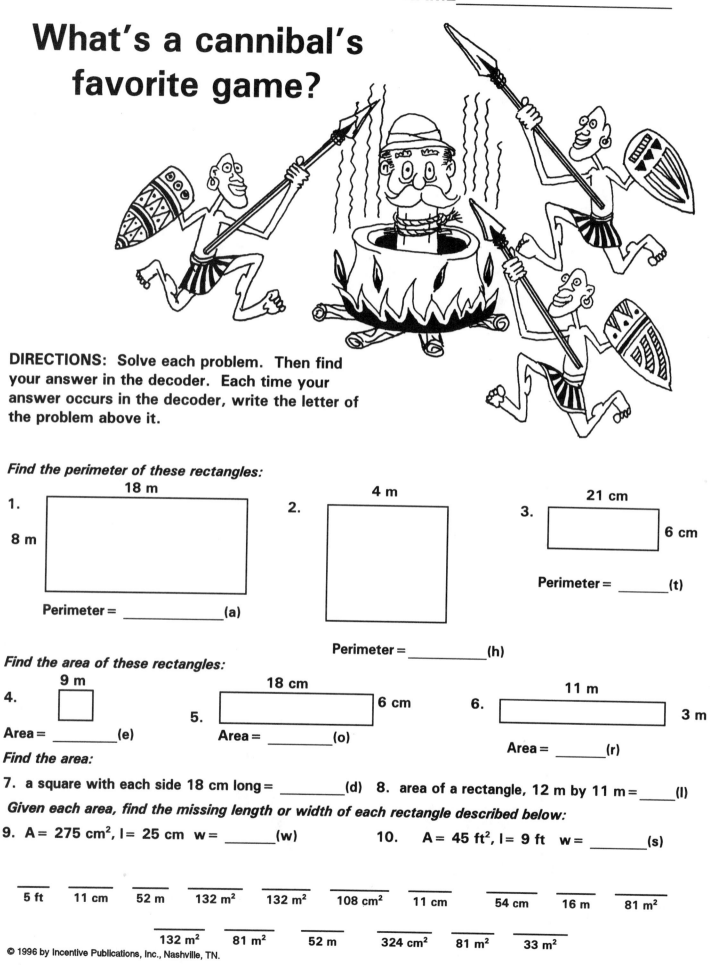

DIRECTIONS: Solve each problem. Then find your answer in the decoder. Each time your answer occurs in the decoder, write the letter of the problem above it.

Find the perimeter of these rectangles:

1.
18 m

8 m

Perimeter = _____ (a)

2.
4 m

Perimeter = _____ (h)

3.
21 cm

6 cm

Perimeter = _____ (t)

Find the area of these rectangles:

4.
9 m

Area = _____ (e)

5.
18 cm

6 cm

Area = _____ (o)

6.
11 m

3 m

Area = _____ (r)

Find the area:

7. a square with each side 18 cm long = _____ (d)   8. area of a rectangle, 12 m by 11 m = _____ (l)

Given each area, find the missing length or width of each rectangle described below:

9. A = 275 cm², l = 25 cm w = _____ (w)   10.   A = 45 ft², l = 9 ft   w = _____ (s)

| 5 ft | 11 cm | 52 m | 132 m² | 132 m² | 108 cm² | 11 cm | 54 cm | 16 m | 81 m² |

| | | 132 m² | 81 m² | 52 m | 324 cm² | 81 m² | 33 m² |

What salad do people prefer when they want privacy?

79

DIRECTIONS: Find the area that is shaded in each of the figures below. Then locate your answer in the decoder. Each time your answer occurs in the decoder, write the letter of the problem above it.

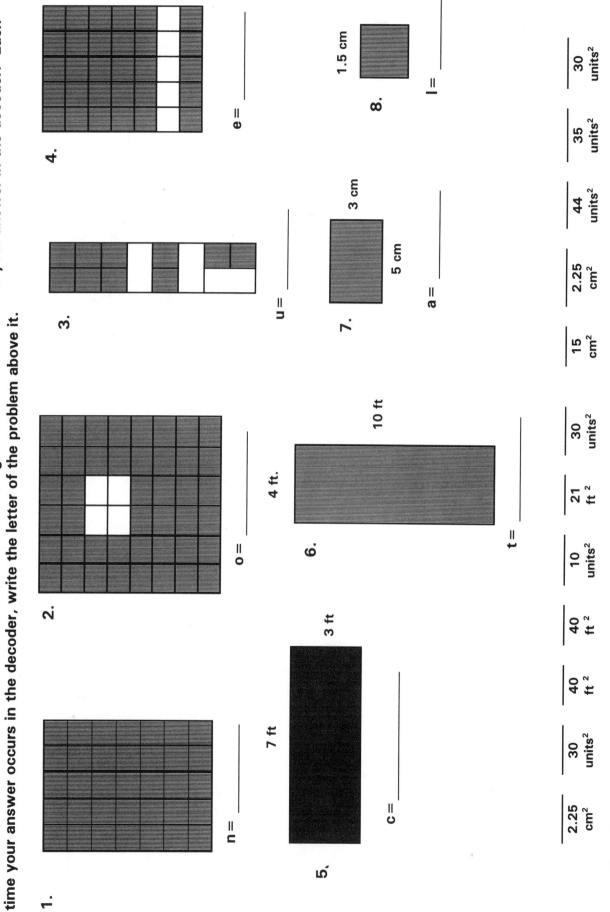

1.

n =

2.

o =

3.

u =

4.

e =

5.

3 ft

7 ft

c =

6.

4 ft.

10 ft

t =

7.

3 cm

5 cm

a =

8.

1.5 cm

l =

2.25 cm²	30 units²	40 ft ²	40 ft ²	10 units²	21 ft ²	30 units²	15 cm²	2.25 cm²	44 units²	35 units²	30 units²

NAME_____

What do you call a successful farmer?

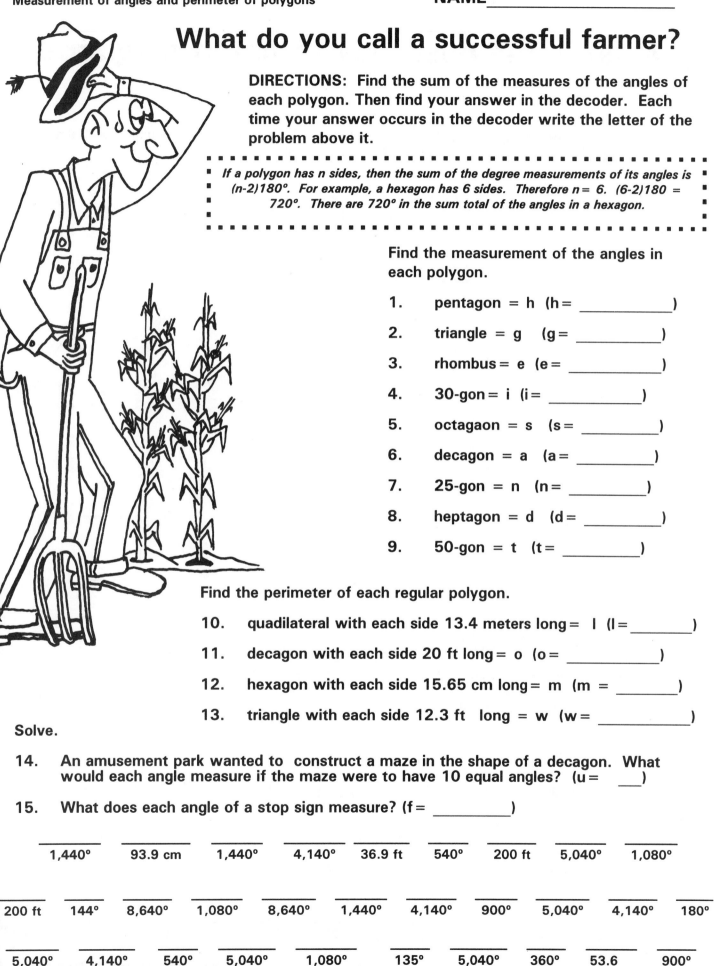

DIRECTIONS: Find the sum of the measures of the angles of each polygon. Then find your answer in the decoder. Each time your answer occurs in the decoder write the letter of the problem above it.

If a polygon has n sides, then the sum of the degree measurements of its angles is (n-2)180°. For example, a hexagon has 6 sides. Therefore n= 6. (6-2)180 = 720°. There are 720° in the sum total of the angles in a hexagon.

Find the measurement of the angles in each polygon.

1.   pentagon = h   (h = _____)

2.   triangle = g   (g = _____)

3.   rhombus = e   (e = _____)

4.   30-gon = i   (i = _____)

5.   octagaon = s   (s = _____)

6.   decagon = a   (a = _____)

7.   25-gon = n   (n = _____)

8.   heptagon = d   (d = _____)

9.   50-gon = t   (t = _____)

Find the perimeter of each regular polygon.

10.   quadilateral with each side 13.4 meters long = l   (l = _____)

11.   decagon with each side 20 ft long = o   (o = _____)

12.   hexagon with each side 15.65 cm long = m   (m = _____)

13.   triangle with each side 12.3 ft   long = w   (w = _____)

Solve.

14.   An amusement park wanted to construct a maze in the shape of a decagon. What would each angle measure if the maze were to have 10 equal angles?   (u = ___)

15.   What does each angle of a stop sign measure? (f = _____)

1,440°	93.9 cm	1,440°	4,140°	36.9 ft	540°	200 ft	5,040°	1,080°

200 ft	144°	8,640°	1,080°	8,640°	1,440°	4,140°	900°	5,040°	4,140°	180°

5,040°	4,140°	540°	5,040°	1,080°	135°	5,040°	360°	53.6	900°

NAME_____

What is the best way to catch a squirrel?

DIRECTIONS: Find the area of each polygon. Then locate your answer in the decoder. Each time your answer occurs in the decoder write the letter of the problem above it.

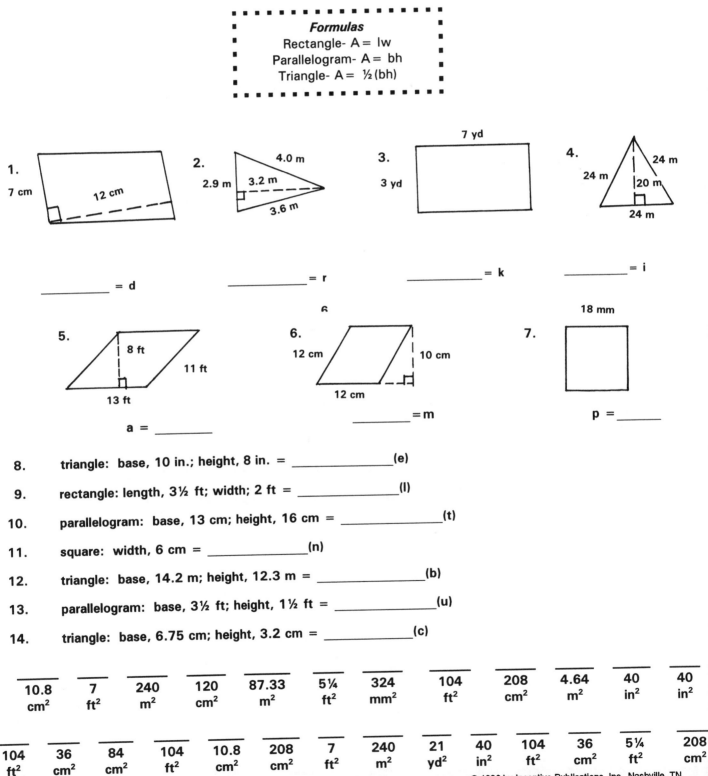

```
                    Formulas
              Rectangle- A = lw
            Parallelogram- A = bh
             Triangle- A = ½(bh)
```

1. 7 cm 12 cm

_____ = d

2. 4.0 m 2.9 m 3.2 m 3.6 m

_____ = r

3. 7 yd 3 yd

_____ = k

4. 24 m 24 m 20 m 24 m

_____ = i

5. 8 ft 11 ft 13 ft

a = _____

6. 12 cm 10 cm 12 cm

_____ = m

7. 18 mm

p = _____

8.   triangle: base, 10 in.; height, 8 in. = _____ **(e)**

9.   rectangle: length, 3½ ft; width; 2 ft = _____ **(l)**

10.   parallelogram: base, 13 cm; height, 16 cm = _____ **(t)**

11.   square: width, 6 cm = _____ **(n)**

12.   triangle: base, 14.2 m; height, 12.3 m = _____ **(b)**

13.   parallelogram: base, 3½ ft; height, 1½ ft = _____ **(u)**

14.   triangle: base, 6.75 cm; height, 3.2 cm = _____ **(c)**

| 10.8 cm² | 7 ft² | 240 m² | 120 cm² | 87.33 m² | 5¼ ft² | 324 mm² | 104 ft² | 208 cm² | 4.64 m² | 40 in² | 40 in² |

| 104 ft² | 36 cm² | 84 cm² | 104 ft² | 10.8 cm² | 208 cm² | 7 ft² | 240 m² | 21 yd² | 40 in² | 104 ft² | 36 cm² | 5¼ ft² | 208 cm² |

What do you call a hired assassin who never serves time?

DIRECTIONS: Find the area of each trapezoid. Then find your answer in the decoder. Each time your answer occurs in the decoder, write the letter of the problem above it.

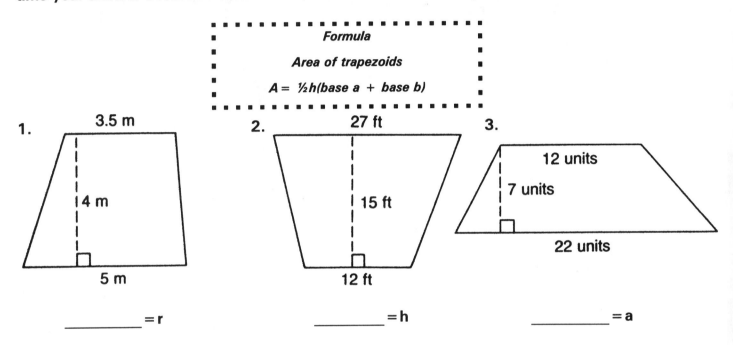

> **Formula**
> **Area of trapezoids**
> $A = \frac{1}{2}h(\text{base } a + \text{base } b)$

1.
3.5 m
4 m
5 m

_____ = r

2.
27 ft
15 ft
12 ft

_____ = h

3.
12 units
7 units
22 units

_____ = a

Find the area of each trapezoid using the measurements given in the chart.

	base (a)	base (b)	height	area	
4.	17 yd	14 yd	8 yd		= (o)
5.	16.3 m	8.4 m	16.2 m		= (n)
6.	5½ yd	4½ yd	8 yd		= (i)
7.	24 in	13 in	14 in		= (m)
8.	5¾ yd	7¾ yd	8 yd		= (t)
9.	4.9 m	2 m	4.6 m		= (x)
10.	19 in	7 in	10 in		= (e)

54 yd²   292.5 ft²   130 in.²

| 130 in² | 15.87 m² | 54 yd² | 130 in² | 17 m² | 259 in² | 40 yd² | 200.07 m² | 119 units² | 54 yd² | 124 yd² | 17 m² |

NAME_____

What did the groom do when his wife made him a marble cake?

DIRECTIONS: Find the circumference of each circle described below. Then find your answer in the decoder. Each time your answer occurs in the decoder write the letter of the problem above it.

$$C = \pi d$$
$$C = 3.14(d)$$

$$C = 2\pi r$$
$$C = 2(3.14)(r)$$

1.
4 m

C = _____ (f)

2.
2 yd

C = _____ (h)

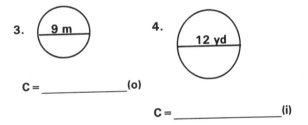

3. 9 m

C = _____ (o)

4. 12 yd

C = _____ (i)

5. 8.1 cm

C = _____ (t)

6. 7 in

C = _____ (k)

7. The radius is 5 miles. C = _____ (e)

8. The diameter is 13.4 km. C = _____ (a)

9. The radius is 3.75 yards. C = _____ (r)

10. The diameter is 6.85 inches. C = _____ (n)

11. The radius is 10.4 cm. C = _____ (g)

12.56 yd	31.4 mi		50.868 cm	28.26 m	28.26 m	21.98 in		37.68 yd	50.868 cm

25.12 m	28.26 m	23.55 mi	65.312 cm	23.55 yd	42.076 km	21.509 in	37.68 yd	50.868 cm	31.4 mi

$A = \pi r^2$

Is there a word in the English language that contains all the vowels?

DIRECTIONS: Find the area of each circle shown. Round your answer to the nearest whole number. Then find your answer in the decoder. Each time your answer occurs in the decoder write the letter of the problem above it.

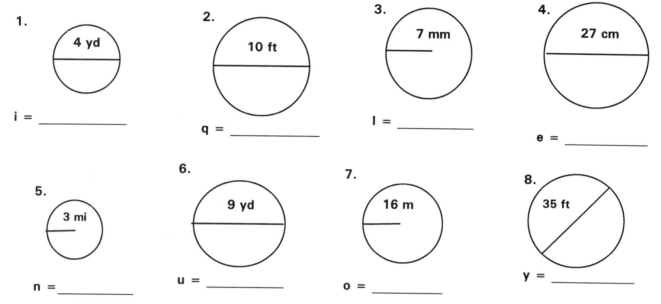

1.

4 yd

i = _____

2.

10 ft

q = _____

3.

7 mm

l = _____

4.

27 cm

e = _____

5.

3 mi

n = _____

6.

9 yd

u = _____

7.

16 m

o = _____

8.

35 ft

y = _____

9. Jupiter, the largest planet in our solar system has a diameter of 88,000 miles. The diameter of the Earth is 7,926 miles. How much larger is Jupiter's diameter than the Earth? _____ = s

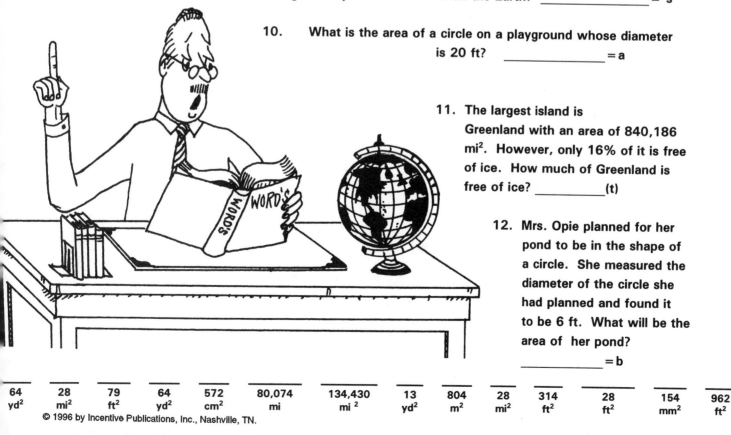

10. What is the area of a circle on a playground whose diameter is 20 ft? _____ = a

11. The largest island is Greenland with an area of 840,186 mi². However, only 16% of it is free of ice. How much of Greenland is free of ice? _____ (t)

12. Mrs. Opie planned for her pond to be in the shape of a circle. She measured the diameter of the circle she had planned and found it to be 6 ft. What will be the area of her pond? _____ = b

64 yd²	28 mi²	79 ft²	64 yd²	572 cm²	80,074 mi	134,430 mi²	13 yd²	804 m²	28 mi²	314 ft²	28 ft²	154 mm²	962 ft²

Name_____

What do you call an astronaut's watch?

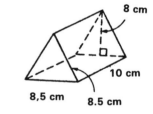

DIRECTIONS: Find the surface area of the rectangular and triangular prisms shown below. Round your answer to the nearest whole number. Then find your answer in the decoder. Each time your answer occurs in the decoder, write the letter of the problem above it.

8 m

1.

r = _____

2.

5 m

7 m

13 m

3.

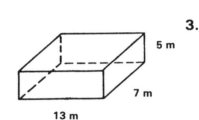

8 cm

10 cm

8,5 cm   8.5 cm

4.

5.1 cm

2.2 cm

1.3 cm

a = _____

5.

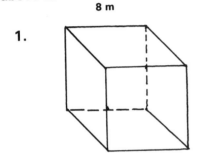

4½ in

7 in   9¾ in

c = _____

i = _____

25.4 cm

6.

u = _____

n = _____

7.

7 m

3 m

2 m

k = _____

8.

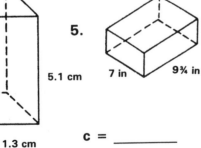

4 cm

5 cm

5 cm

t = _____

9.

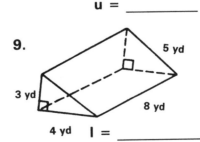

5 yd

3 yd

8 yd

4 yd   l = _____

41 cm²	108 yd²	3,871 cm²	323 cm²	41 cm²	384 m²	63 cm²	382 m²	279 in²	82 m²

Which illness was common to the Brontosaurus?

DIRECTIONS: Find each square or the square root. Then find your answer in the decoder. Each time your answer occurs in the decoder write the letter of the problem above it.

Find each square root.

1. $\sqrt{81}$ = _____ (i)

2. $\sqrt{256}$ = _____ (a)

3. $-\sqrt{121}$ = _____ (o)

4. $-\sqrt{100}$ = _____ (e)

5. $\sqrt{361}$ = _____ (t)

Find the square of each number.

6. 8 = _____ (r)

7. 13 = _____ (h)

8. 12 = _____ (n)

9. 16 = _____ (d)

10. 32 = _____ (s)

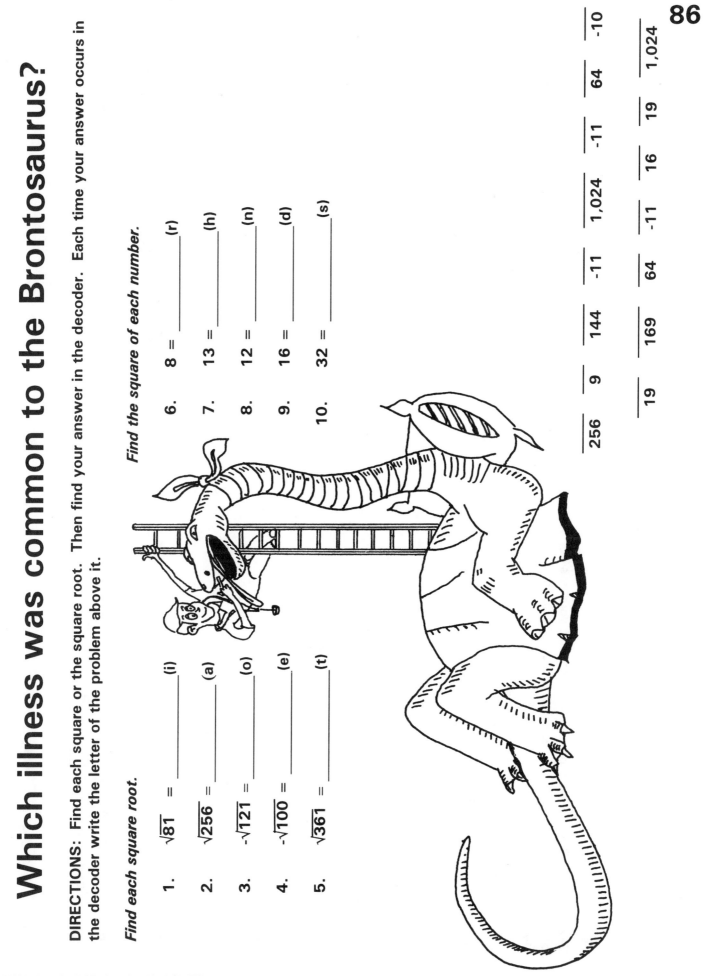

256	9	144	-11	1,024	-11	16	-11	64	-10

19	169	64	-11	19	1,024

NAME _____

Reviewing polynomials

What illness do you get from overeating?

DIRECTIONS: Solve each problem and then find your answer in the decoder. Each time your answer occurs, write the letter of the problem above it.

Find the degree of each polynominal.

1. $19b^2c^3 - 14bc^4$ _____ (a)

2. $4x^2y$ _____ (m)

3. $4w + z^2$ _____ (i)

Find each sum.

4. $(4x + 1) + (3x + 1) = c$ c= _____

5. $(5y - 7x) + (6y + 8x) = u$ u= _____

Find the difference.

6. $(5q^2 + 11) - (5q^2 - 6) = o$ o= _____

7. $(d^2 + 7d + 3) - (d^2 + 7d + 3) = r$ r= _____

Simplify.

8. $(-2c)^3 = y$ y= _____

9. $4x(x^2y)^3 = k$ k= _____

10. $(x^3)^3 = h$ h= _____

Find each product.

11. $-3x(x + 6) = s$ s= _____

12. $10(3c - 4d) = t$ t= _____

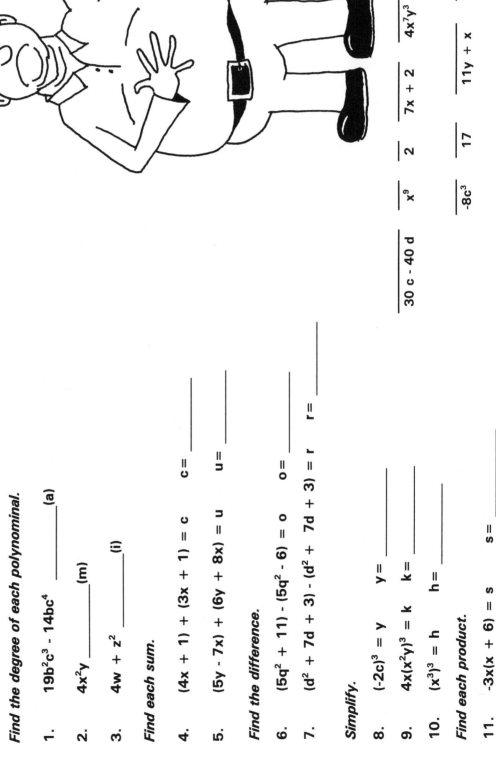

$\overline{30\ c - 40\ d}$ $\overline{x^9}$ $\overline{2}$ $\overline{7x + 2}$ $\overline{4x^7y^3}$ $\overline{30c - 40d}$ $\overline{17}$

$\overline{-8c^3}$ $\overline{17}$ $\overline{11y + x}$ $\overline{0}$

$\overline{-3x^2 - 18x}$ $\overline{30c - 40d}$ $\overline{17}$ $\overline{3}$ $\overline{5}$ $\overline{7x + 2}$ $\overline{x^9}$

ANSWER KEY

Page 1 1. 18   2. 22   3. $9   4. $8   5. 4,260   6. 102   7. 60   8. 0.9   9. 14   10. 15   11. 68   (A smile that bursts)

Page 2 1. 7   2. 10   3. 18   4. 8   5. 96   6. 5   7. 225   8. 36   9. 25   10. 1   11. 21   12. 44   (They are always on their tows)

Page 3 1. 10   2. 17   3. 150   4. 33   5. 12   6. 14   7. 15.41   8. 16   9. 215   10. 30   11. 20   12. 155   13. 15
(One might be a lion and one might be a cheetah)

Page 4 1. 16   2. -12   3. -18   4. 48   5. 17   6. -16   7. 22   8. 29   9. 13   10. -24   11. -2   12. -10   13. -17   14. -4
(The sun rose and the wind blue)

Page 5 1. -25   2. 16   3. 64   4. 8   5. 9   6. -4   7. 32   8. 33   9. 0   10. 1   11. -60   12. -70   13. -3
(Hair today gone tomorrow)

Page 6 1. -7   2. 3   3. -39   4. -14   5. 0   6. -15   7. 53   8. -38   9. -9   10. -80   11. 1   12. -3   (In case they get a hole in one)

Page 7 Alabama- 139°   Alaska- 180°   California- 179°   Georgia- 129°   Montana- 187°   Nevada- 172°   New York- 160°   Tennessee-145°
Utah- 186°   Hawaii- 88°   1. Montana   2. Utah   3. Hawaii   4. Alaska   5. California

Page 8 1. 43, 52, 61   2. 13, 6, -1   3. -19, -27, -35   4. 28, 39, 52   5. 8.79, 10.13, 11.47   6. -70, -55, -40   7. $5\frac{7}{12}$, $6\frac{1}{3}$, $7\frac{1}{12}$ 8. 1.82, 1.76, 1.7   9. 0, 4, 8   10. 243, 729, 2,187   11. $-2\frac{1}{4}$, $-2\frac{7}{12}$, $-2\frac{11}{12}$ 12. 32, 64, 128   13. -1,024, 4,096 -16,384

Page 9 1. -162   2. -192   3. 140   4. -850   5. 77   6. -512   7. 72   8. 32   9. -210   10. 84   11. -126   12. 90   13. -108
(Then it would be a foot)

Page 10 1. -12   2. 7   3. 49   4. -8   5. -5   6. -7   7. 4   8. -16   9. 20   10. 6   11. -18   (Out of sight out of mind)

Page 11 1. -9   2. -130   3. -5   4. 24   5. 120   6. -4   7. 136   8. 2   9. 8   10. -8   11. -6   12. -162   13. 20
(The Holy Roman Umpire)

Page 12 1. 23   2. -11   3. 15   4. -59   5. $8,291   6. $618   7. -37   8. 43   9. -20   10. 21   11. -27   12. -46   13. -26
14. -75   (Both are in the middle of water)

Page 13 1. 48   2. 19   3. -4   4. -5   5. -23   6. -85   7. -37   8. 34   9. 58   10. 35   11. $113   13. $375   14. -350
(I have his Gettysburg Address right here)

Page 14 1. -8   2. 12   3. -15   4. -16   5. -13   6. 13   7. 8   8. 4   9. 7   10. 84   11. $75   (The pound cake)

Page 15 1. -147   2. -195   3. -256   4. -9936   5. 476   6. 48   7. 90   8. -768   9. 20   10. 4   11. -12   (Table of continents)

Page 16 1. 16   2. 27   3. 4,096   4. 1   5. 216   6. 343   7. 121   8. 10,000   9. 625   10. 1,728   11. 64
(They haven't got any body)

Page 17 1. 100,000   2. 1,000,000   3. $-27b^4c^3$ 4. $42w^5z^5$ 5. $18w^2z^3$ 6. b^2c^3 7. $6w^3z^5$ 8. 14,400   9. 512   10. b^8c^2
11. w^{10} 12. $4z^6$ 13. 1,000   (When you are over the hump)

Page 18 1. $\frac{1}{4bc}$ 2. $\frac{b}{-3c}$ 3. $\frac{3}{4c}$ 4. b^2 5. $\frac{1}{2a}$ 6. $\frac{-5b^2}{2}$ 7. bc^4 8. b^2c 9. $2c^2$ (They had a chute out)

Page 19 FACTORS MAY VARY.   1. composite   2. composite   3. composite   4. composite   5. prime   6. prime   7. composite
8. prime   9. composite   10. prime   11. composite   12. prime   13. prime   14. composite   15. prime   16. composite
17. composite   18. prime   19. composite   20. composite

Page 20 ORDER OF FACTORS MAY VARY.   1. -1 x 5 x 2 x 11   2. 11 x 13 x r x r x s   3. -1 x 3 x 2 x 2 x 3 x 2 x 2
4. -1 x 2 x 2 x 2 x 2 x t x t x s x s   5. 5 x 5 x 5 x 2 x 2 x b x c x c   6. -1 x 5 x 7 x 2 x 2   7. 3 x 17 x j x j x k
8. -1 x 5 x 5 x 5 x 5 x a x a x b x b   9. 2 x 7 x 7   10. -1 x 2 x 2 x 2 x 2 x 2 x 2 x 5 x 5 x g x g   11. 13 x 13 x 3 x 3
12. 5 x 5 x 5 x 5 x 2 x 2 x 2 x 2

Page 21 1. 1   2. x   3. 20   4. 30x   5. 5   6. 5z   7. 12   8. 3   9. 16   10. 6op   11. 36   12. 7   13. 33
(Thanks I will never part with this)

Page 22 1. 35   2. 60k   3. 36   4. $30p^2$ 5. $60p^2$ 6. 108   7. $105j^2$ 8. 48j   9. 51   10. $84k^2$ 11. 100   12. $120k^2$
(Their Bach is worse than their bite)

Page 23 1. 15, 30, $\frac{1}{2}$ 2. 12, 72, $\frac{2}{3}$ 3. 2, 1,240, $\frac{20}{31}$ 4. 6, 36, $\frac{2}{3}$ 5. 18, 216, $\frac{3}{4}$ 6. 8, 960, $\frac{8}{15}$ 7. 14, 336, $\frac{3}{8}$ 8. 8, 1216, $\frac{8}{19}$
9. 8, 168, $\frac{3}{7}$ 10. 3, 60, $\frac{4}{5}$ 11. 4, 180, $\frac{5}{9}$ 12. 4, 48, $\frac{3}{4}$ 13. 5, 75, $\frac{3}{5}$ 14. 4, 160, $\frac{5}{8}$ 15. 9, 54, $\frac{2}{3}$ 16. 10, 240, $\frac{3}{8}$
17. 11, 132, $\frac{3}{4}$ 18. 4, 60, $\frac{3}{5}$

Page 24 1. 29   2. 16   3. 99   4. 49   5. 60   6. 2   7. 12   8. 66   9. 97   10. 54   11. 11   12. 5   13. 18   14. 72
15. 96   16. 37   17. 64   (butterfly, brown rat, rhinoceros beetle, anaconda)

Page 25 1. $\frac{3}{4}$ 2. $\frac{9}{11}$ 3. $\frac{1}{2}$ 4. $\frac{6}{7}$ 5. $\frac{3v}{10}$ 6. $\frac{3a}{5}$ 7. $\frac{2}{3}$ 8. $\frac{2g}{3}$ 9. $\frac{3}{7}$ 10. $\frac{8s}{r}$ 11. $\frac{16m}{21n}$ (It is not my fault)

Page 26 1. $\frac{3}{5}$ 2. $-\frac{8}{111}$ 3. $\frac{5}{11}$ 4. $-\frac{19}{20}$ 5. $5\frac{3}{4}$ 6. $\frac{54}{125}$ 7. $\frac{1}{10}$ 8. $-\frac{32}{33}$ 9. $\frac{4}{5}$ (Mount Everest)

Page 27 1. 54.3 2. 54.4 3. 82 4. 64.1 5. 64.19 6. 81.14 7. 81.24 8. 7,016.32 9. 971.541 10. 971.693
11. 2.198   12. 2.982 13. 54.494 (It was free for the axing)

Page 28 1. 750 2. 14 3. 47 4. 24 5. 2 6. 15 7. 18 8. 36 9. 32 10. 9 11. 11 (One word leads to another)

Page 29 1. -28 2. 8.604 3. -43.33 4. 5.067 5. 4.4 6. 24.59 7. 45.627 8. -8.1 9. -37.12 10. 98.54 11. -3.17
12. 7.8 13. 3.997 14. 6.55 (A mountain that keeps getting sick)

Page 30 3/17 - $447.79   3/17 - $257.04   3/18 - $207.04   3/19 - $417.84   3/21 - $358.19   3/22 - $147.34
3/23 - $617.34

Page 31 1. 12,000 lb 2. 1 year 3. 1½ ton 4. 13 gal 5. 12 pt 6. 2 mi 7. 1,760 yd 8. 8 ft 2 in 9. 5 gal 2 qt
10. 8 yd 1 ft 11. 8 ft 3 in 12. 1 gal 2 qt 13. 4 qt (He wanted to see antifreeze)

Page 32 1. $0.8\overline{3}$ 2. 0.76 3. 2.875 4. $1.91\overline{6}$ 5. $0.41\overline{6}$ 6. 0.4375 7. $0.\overline{21}$ 8. 0.6
(A quarter to two)

Page 33 1. -0.448 2. -30.1 3. -168.1 4. 2.4009 5. 56.03 6. 328 7. 18.108 8. -237.82 9. 131.4 10. -7.3438
11. 33.84 (Because it is quite a strain)

Page 34 1. 10.22 2. 60 3. 0.065 4. 3.6 5. 2.81 6. -7.5 7. 2.5 8. 0.579 9. 0.01 10. -8.9 11. -809 12. 9
13. -0.32 14. -0.53 (Toucan can stay for the price of one)

Page 35 1. Sept. 18 - 31   Sept. 27 - 27.7   Oct. 3 - 27.8   Oct. 10 - 31.2   1. 29.8 2. Answers will vary.

Page 36 a. .417 b. .667 c. .367   Gwynn - .394   Bagwell - .368   O'Neil - .359   Belle - .357   Thomas - .353
Lofton - .349   Boggs - .342   Alou - .339   Morris - .335   Mitchell - .326   1. Cincinnati, New York, Cleveland
2. .352, They are the same.

Page 37 1. 7,300 2. 96,430 3. -0.0000316 4. -2.104 5. -311,000 6. -13.694 7. 0.000708 8. 47,000
9. 894,000,000,000 10. 340 11. 31,100 12. -0.073 13. 136.94 14. -80 (They are celebrating a bisontennial)

Page 38 1. $\frac{1}{49}$ 2. $-5\frac{1}{3}$ 3. $\frac{17}{27}$ 4. $12\frac{24}{25}$ 5. $\frac{1}{4}$ 6. 150   7. 3 8. $-\frac{3}{4}$ 9. $\frac{5}{16}$ 10. $\frac{2}{3}$ 11. $\frac{z}{x}$ 12. $\frac{4}{9}$
13. $-6\frac{2}{3}$ 14. 5 15. 8 16. $-\frac{5}{16}$ 17. 4 (They like to keep things under wraps)

Page 39 1. 5 2. -12 3. 20 4. -288 5. 6 6. -33 7. -9 8. 72 9. 8 10. -480 11. 552 (I owe nothing for I
ate nothing)

Page 40 1. 11 2. 20 3. 4 4. 19 5. -32 6. 180 7. 3 8. 26 9. 14 (A person who snores)

Page 41 1. 32 2. 21 3. 8 4. 49 5. 15 6. 9 7. 1 8. 18 9. 10 10. 0 11. 45 (Pledge of allegiance)

Page 42 1. 16 2. 1 3. 8 4. 12 5. -2 6. 10 7. -73 8. -2.8 9. -5 10. -14 11. -12 12. 3 (Now I herd everything)

Page 43 1. -13 2. 2.6 3. 5 4. -4 5. -3.5 6. 3 7. 16 8. 1.5 9. 54 10 -1.5 11. 6 12. 1 13. 32 14. -6
(His grades were below C level)

Page 44 Answers will vary.

Page 45 1. 3 2. 2,900 3. 0.38 4. 3.821 5. 2 6. 12,000 7. 0.075 8. 400 9. 20 10. 3.752 11. 0.0075
12. 65,000 13. 0.3821 14. 3,752 15. 38 (It is when your tang gets toungled)

Page 46. 1. 800 2. 4,000 3. 0.014 4. 0.0098 5. 0.12 6. 0.0803 7. 400 8. 0.803 9. 1.4 10. 9,800,000 11. 0.4
12. 40,000 13. 120 (Too wise you are, too wise you be, I see you are too wise for me)

Page 47 1. -5 2. -7 3. 2 4. -1 5. -2 6. 0 7. 5 8. 1 (B C ing you)

Page 48 - 49 Graphs will vary.

Page 50

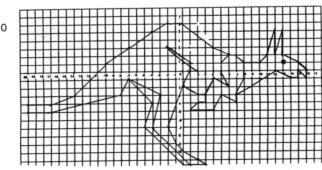

Page 51 - 52   Individual student graphs will vary.

Page 53 Area designs will vary.

Page 54   1. x= 1 y= 2, x= 2 y= 0, x= 3 y= -2, x= 4 y= -4   2. x= -1 y= 0, x= 0 y= 1,   x= 3 y= 4,   x= 5
 y= 6   3. x = -3 y = 0,   x = 0 y = 2,   x = 3 y = 4,   x = 6 y= 6   4. x= 0 y= -1,   x = 1 y = -½,   x = 2 y= 0,   x = 3 y= ½

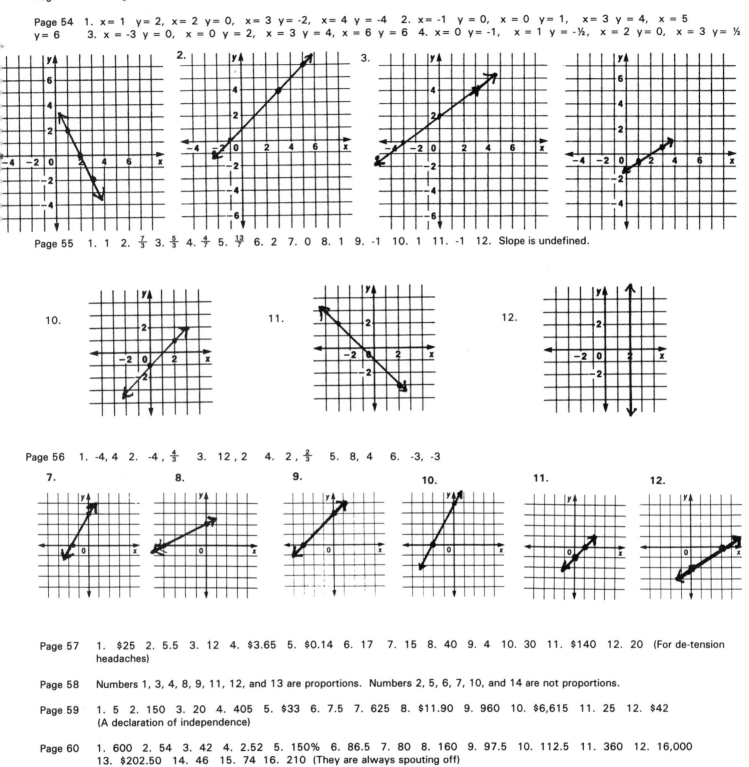

Page 55   1. 1   2. $\frac{7}{3}$ 3. $\frac{5}{3}$ 4. $\frac{4}{7}$ 5. $\frac{13}{7}$ 6. 2   7. 0   8. 1   9. -1   10. 1   11. -1   12. Slope is undefined.

Page 56   1. -4, 4   2. -4 , $\frac{4}{3}$ 3. 12 , 2   4. 2, $\frac{2}{3}$ 5. 8, 4   6. -3, -3

Page 57   1. $25   2. 5.5   3. 12   4. $3.65   5. $0.14   6. 17   7. 15   8. 40   9. 4   10. 30   11. $140   12. 20   (For de-tension
headaches)

Page 58   Numbers 1, 3, 4, 8, 9, 11, 12, and 13 are proportions. Numbers 2, 5, 6, 7, 10, and 14 are not proportions.

Page 59   1. 5   2. 150   3. 20   4. 405   5. $33   6. 7.5   7. 625   8. $11.90   9. 960   10. $6,615   11. 25   12. $42
(A declaration of independence)

Page 60   1. 600   2. 54   3. 42   4. 2.52   5. 150%   6. 86.5   7. 80   8. 160   9. 97.5   10. 112.5   11. 360   12. 16,000
13. $202.50   14. 46   15. 74   16. 210   (They are always spouting off)

Page 61   1. 4.5   2. 5   3. 0.75   4. $3   5. 1,600   6. 1   7. 15   8. 100   9. 5%   10. 75%   11. 10%   12. 25%
3. 20%   14. 60%   (It never speaks until it is tolled)

Page 62   1. 362   2. 70   3. 20%   4. 12   5. 272   6. 36   7. 1.6%   8. 80   9. $12,500   10. $7.36   11. 8%   12. 30
(Look at the orange marmalade)

Page 63   (These answers may vary.) 1. 33%, $\frac{1}{3}$, less   2. 90%, $\frac{9}{10}$, more   3. 20%, $\frac{1}{5}$, less   4. 100%, $\frac{1}{1}$, more   5. 60%, $\frac{3}{5}$, less
6. 75%, $\frac{3}{4}$, less   7. 87½%, $\frac{7}{8}$, less   8. 25%, ¼, more   9. 37½%, $\frac{3}{8}$, more   10. 12½%, $\frac{1}{8}$, less   11. 70%, $\frac{7}{10}$, more
12. 50%, ½, more

Page 64   1. 34%   2. 91$\frac{2}{3}$%   3. 120%   4. 250%   5. 20.4%   6. 7%   7. 0.6%   8. 104.3%   9. $\frac{12}{25}$ 10. $\frac{1}{40}$ 11. $\frac{7}{8}$ 12. 0.12
13. 0.33$\frac{1}{3}$ 14. 0.135   (Someone tickling the ivories)

Page 65 1. $472.50 2. $78 3. $99 4. $262.50 5. $56 6. $72,000 7. $15,000 8. $457.20 9. 40%
10. 27% 11. 31% 12. 34% 13. 33% (Telephone, television, and tell a gossip)

Page 66 1. 15% 2. 5% 3. 13% 4. 11% 5. 80% 6. 50% 7. 34% 8. 10% 9. 20% 10. 75%
11. 26% 12. 27% (There is never any change in it)

Page 67 1. Frequency- 3, 0, 3, 1, 1, 1, 3 2. 100 3. 55 4. 3 5. 9 6. 3 7. 79 8. 6, 9, 13, 11 6, 3, 2 9. 50
10. 11 to 13 11. 12%

Page 68 1. 3.9 2. 10.56 3. 1.0341 4. 67 5. 1.41 6. 5.7 7. 74.2 8. 10.48 9. 163 10. 92 11. 97
12. 91.8 13. 1.8 (They feel for the pine trees that pine)

Page 69 Cory- 869, 79, C; Mark- 797, 72, D; Nathan- 710, 65, F; Forrest- 1,071, 97, A; Angela- 951, 86, B; Maria- 769,
70, D; Earl- 842, 77, C; Kyung- 1,097, 100, A; Jeff- 876, 80, C; Dementra- 1,016, 92, A; Jenny- 845, 77, C;
Sinbad- ,032, 94, A. 1. 80 2. 77, 83 3. 85, 85, 80 4. Nathan, Maria 5. Extra credit(Possible answer) 6. 5, Yes;
His average would have been 71 and he would have passed the class. 7. Her grade would have changed from D to B.

Page 70 1. 9 2. 12 3. 6 4. 9

Page 71 1. 7,776 2. 24 3. 20 4. 18 5. 288 6. 256 7. 15 (With a low ha)

Page 72 Answers will vary.

Page 73 $\frac{1}{6}$ is the probability for each color.

Page 74 1. obtuse, 101° 2. acute, 25° 3. acute, 32° 4. obtuse, 158° 5. right, 90° 6. acute, 9° 7. acute, 76°
8. obtuse, 130° 9. acute, 14° (A rubber bandit)

Page 75 1. 48° + 80° + 52° = 180° 2. 90° + 46° + 44° = 180° 3. 110° + 40° + 30° = 180° 4. 110° + 70° + 70° + 110° 360°
5. 4 x 90° = 360° 6. 51° + 128° + 142° + 39° = 360° 7. 70° + 110° + 70° + 110° = 360°

Page 76 Drawings and answers will vary.

Page 77 Answers will vary.

Page 78 1. 52 m 2. 16 m 3. 54 cm 4. 81 m² 5. 108 cm² 6. 33 m² 7. 324 cm² 8. 132 m² 9. 11 cm   10. 5 ft
(Swallow the leader)

Page 79 1. 35 units² 2. 44 units² 3. 10 units² 4. 30 units² 5. 21 ft² 6. 40 ft² 7. 15 cm² 8. 2.25 cm² (Lettuce alone)

Page 80 1. 540° 2. 180° 3. 360° 4. 5,040° 5. 1,080° 6. 1,440° 7. 4,140° 8. 900° 9. 8,640° 10. 53.6 m
11. 200 ft 12. 93.9 cm 13. 36.9 ft 14. 144° 15, 135° (A man who is outstanding in his field)

Page 81 1. 84 cm² 2. 4.64 m² 3. 21 yd² 4. 240 m² 5. 104 ft² 6. 120 cm² 7. 324 mm² 8. 40 in² 9. 7 ft²
10. 208 cm² 11. 36 cm² 12. 87.33 m² 13. 5.25 ft² 14. 10.8 cm² (Climb up a tree and act like a nut)

Page 82 1. 17 m² 2. 292.5 ft² 3. 119 units² 4. 124 yd² 5. 200.07 m² 6. 40 yd² 7. 259 in² 8. 54 yd²
9. 15.87 m² 10. 130 in² (The exterminator)

Page 83 1. 25.12 m 2. 12.56 yd 3. 28.26 m 4. 37.68 yd 5. 50.868 cm 6. 21.98 in 7. 31. 4 miles 8. 42.076 km
9. 23.55 yd 10. 21.509 in 11. 65. 312 cm (He took it for granite)

Page 84 1. 13 yd² 2. 79 ft² 3. 154 mm² 4. 572 cm² 5. 28 mi² 6. 64 yd² 7. 804 m² 8. 962 ft² 9. 80,074 miles
10. 314 ft² 11. 134,430 m² 12. 28 ft² (Unquestionably)

Page 85 1. 384 m² 2. 382 m² 3. 323 cm² 4. 41 cm² 5. 279 in² 6. 3,872 cm² 7. 82 m² 8. 63 cm²   9. 108 yd²
(A lunar tick)

Page 86 1. 9 2. 16 3. -11 4. -10 5. 19 6. 64 7. 169 8. 144 9. 256 10. 1,024   (Dino-sore throats)

Page 87 1. 5 2. 3 3. 2 4. 7x + 2 5. 11y + x 6. 17 7. 0 8. -8c³ 9. 4x⁷y³ 10. x⁹ 11. -3x² - 18x
12. 30c - 40d (Thick to your stomach)